BOB HOPE'S BUNGALOW:
Tales From The Typing Trenches

Written By
Carol Shaw

Orlando, Florida

BOB HOPE'S BUNGALOW: *Tales From The Typing Trenches*
Copyright ©2022 Carol Shaw. All Rights Reserved.

No part of this book may be reproduced in any form or by any means, electronic, mechanical, digital, photocopying or recording, except for the inclusion in a review, without permission in writing from the publisher.

This book is an independent work of research and commentary and is not sponsored, authorized or endorsed by, or otherwise affiliated with, any motion picture studio or production company affiliated with the films discussed herein. All uses of the name, image, and likeness of any individuals, and all copyrights and trademarks referenced in this book, are for editorial purposes and are pursuant of the Fair Use Doctrine.

The views and opinions of individuals quoted in this book do not necessarily reflect those of the author.

The promotional photographs and publicity materials reproduced herein are in the author's private collection (unless noted otherwise). These images date from the original release of the films and were released to media outlets for publicity purposes.
Cover Illustration by Oisin McGillion Hughes.

Published in the USA by
BearManor Media
1317 Edgewater Dr. #110
Orlando, FL 32804
www.BearManorMedia.com

Softcover Edition
ISBN-10:
ISBN-13: 978-1-62933-886-6

Printed in the United States of America

ACKNOWLEDGEMENTS

I'm extremely grateful and thankful to writer extraordinaire, Julie G. Beers, for all her support, guidance and belief in my writing ability. She has shown me what it truly means to be a great friend!

I'd also like to express my deepest thanks to my favorite artist and author, Steve J. Beers, for providing his fabulous caricature of Bob Hope and myself on the cover, as well as his continued support of my writing.

Chapter 1

THE BOB HOPE UNVEILING

Bob Hope stepped out on the balcony next to his agent Mark Anthony and looked at me as I rushed down the stairs.

"Can you find Armando? I need to talk to him!" yelled Mr. Hope to me.

Armando was Mr. Hope's all around handyman who worked at the house.

I stopped and turned toward Mr. Hope's voice and said, "I'll get him for you, Mr......"

That's when I froze, along with all time as we know it. Butterflies fluttering near the geranium pots on the balcony froze. Birds flying in the sky froze. A jet plane overhead froze in mid-air. The sounds of all neighborhood lawn mowers stopped. It was unnaturally quiet.

You could hear a pin drop as I was staring up at Bob Hope. I realized this was my first look at Mr. Hope and had hoped it would be memorable. And it was! A little too memorable.

I was so shocked at the vision of seeing Bob Hope that I couldn't get the last word out. My mouth was wide open in a perfect circle as I stood there frozen staring up at Mr. Hope. Not because it was *the* Bob Hope. *Au contraire*! I had seen movie stars before. No, this was different.

The Bob Hope I was looking at was almost completely NAKED! A naked 80-year-old Bob Hope! Holy cow! It was a double whammy!

Bob stood there in all his glory wearing just a pair of white skivvies. Actually, they were teeny-weeny panties. Tight ones. Really tight Bikini panties. I could see everything and more than I wanted to see. He wasn't skinny by any stretch of the imagination and had all this curly white hair covering his body. What a sight to behold.

That was the last thing I needed to see at 9:30 in the morning. I was stunned to say the least.

And the other funny thing, I had never seen an 80-year-old so unapologetically proud of his nakedness. Shoot, I had never seen any of my former bosses naked before and they were way younger than eighty! I guess that happens in show biz. No one cares if you're dressed, undressed, half dressed, or wearing Prada.

"Armando's probably out back," offered Mr. Hope, oblivious to my reaction of him, like this happens every day.

"Oh," I whispered, still frozen in place. That was the only word that I could get out. But I didn't move. I *couldn't* move. My eyes ran up and down Mr. Hope's naked chunky frame as he stood there. I just couldn't believe what my eyes were telling me.

Finally, he looked down at himself and apparently picked up on my uncomfortableness because he moved back and half-hid himself behind the door. So I was now treated to seeing half of Bob Hope, specifically his hairy leg and arm, straddling the door frame.

"That way," he awkwardly gestured to the right.

I pulled myself together and croaked, "I'll get Armando for you."

BOB HOPE'S BUNGALOW: TALES FROM THE TYPING TRENCHES

As I turned back, I slipped on the bottom step and almost fell but caught myself just in time. Then I started running down the driveway as fast as I could.

I could hear faint laughter behind me and glanced back.

Mr. Hope and Mark Anthony were watching me and grinning like Cheshire cats at my uncomfortableness. Yes, that was real funny, guys. Frighten the new girl! Welcome to Hollywood! I wondered, was it going to be like this every day?

Oh good grief, yes… and more!

Bob Hope was born in England on May 29, 1903. He started in Vaudeville in 1921 which spanned an almost eighty year or so career in Hollywood, or "Hollyweird," as I fondly called it.

Bob was loved by all back in the day and made a reputation for himself when he emceed the Academy Awards show. Only Bob Hope can say he stood before the Academy's podium as Master of Ceremonies nineteen times. That's a record. He often joked that he should be given an Oscar. The Academy finally relented one year and gave him a bigger-than-life golden Oscar which he put in the corner of his den. Bob Hope was funny, sharp, and topical in his joke telling.

Towards the end, he relied on his staff of writers who took up the gauntlet and somehow infused themselves into his arsenal of jokes. It was a skill. Some have it on a small scale, and others have it big time. The writers of jokes, gags, one-liners, and snappy comebacks truly amaze me. How on earth can you come up with jokes that fast?

Mr. Hope learned this skill at humor way back in the days of Vaudeville and never looked back. He was America's funnyman, even if he had been born in England.

Everyone likes to laugh and this book is dedicated to doing just that. I cannot repeat the thousands upon thousands of jokes he and his writers came up with over the years, but I can give you a flavor of what it was like being a fish out of water, as I was, and tossed into the wacky world of Bob Hope.

Come along with me. I'm going to share some of my own personal story as it was back in the early 1980s and intermix it with what it really was like working for a celebrity known for his sense of humor as well as the good, the bad, and the ugly.

No, those were NOT his writers.

Chapter 2

BEGINNINGS

My story of working for Bob Hope began one early California morning in 1983.

I had just picked up the Glendale newspaper from the front lawn and turned to go back inside the two-story apartment building. Blocking me was my tall landlady, Gloria, all five-foot-nine of her. She leaned toward me and was about two inches away from my head. It was a little too close for me, but she had a big grin on her face. She was one of those friendly Tennessee gals and had a twang when she spoke.

"I've found the perfect man for you," she announced triumphantly.

I backed up. She was leaning even closer into my "space," and it was unnerving.

"I really need to find a job before I look for a man," I said.

She leaned in closer and whispered quietly, "You'll change your mind when you see his picture."

She jammed the Polaroid she had in her hand into my face.

I looked at the Polaroid and involuntarily did a double take.

The picture was of a long-haired guy in tight jeans. Sort of cute. Was he a musician? He looked like he was stoned.

"Oh my God," I said softly, trying to place where I had seen him before.

"Yes, my son is *that* good of a catch," she said crowing proudly.

"Is he in a band?" I asked, because I was into the latest music of the day.

"No, Chuck likes to work alone. Take another look."

She jammed the picture forward again so I could see better.

"And you said you would meet him. Well, here he is."

"I guess it couldn't hurt to just meet," I said examining the photo.

What got me was his unibrow. I just couldn't stop staring at it. That was one big, hairy eyebrow floating across his face like a centipede.

Note to self: Bring scissors on the date.

"Sexy, right?" she said with pride. Did she mean Chuck or the centipede?

"He's growing on me," I said. Growing like a fungus, was what I really meant.

I smiled back at her. What else was there to say? I didn't want to hurt anyone's feelings.

"Chuck will be at your door at 7:00 p.m. Saturday night," she declared. "Wear a dress. Chuck likes legs."

I involuntarily looked down at my white legs.

"Okay," I said as I swallowed hard. How was I going to get out of this?

Chuck looked like a hillbilly straight out of *Deliverance* (1972). I felt like the character Ned Beatty played in *Deliverance*, only shorter.

I went inside my apartment shutting the door on the world, and locking it several times.

The refrigerator was close by. I opened it and peered in. I needed a drink. Hard liquor, preferably. All I could find was an apple juice box which I took. I moved to the living room and sat down on the floor spreading out the newspaper. I found the Want Ads section and pulled it out.

As I laid on my back on the floor, I held the newspaper ads directly above me. The bold-capped headline of a HELP WANTED ad caught my eye. It could have been the caps, but it was the words that actually drew me in. I flipped over and sat up. I pulled the paper toward me for a closer look.

It wasn't like any other secretarial ad I had ever read. It was promising. It was oozing a come-hither finger pointing directly at me. SECRETARY NEEDED MUST HAVE SENSE OF HUMOR was the first line of the help wanted ad.

I carefully tore out the ad from the paper. Then I re-read it over and over. It was a curious help wanted ad.

This particular period in time was the early eighties. There was no Twitter, no Facebook, and definitely no Apple cell phones. In 1983 there was a gigantic Motorola mobile phone that cost around $3,000, but it couldn't text, take a picture, or go online. The Internet was not yet created. In six year's time the World Wide Web would be introduced from a twinkling of an idea by a computer programmer in Switzerland which would have a burgeoning demand. But no one knew that in 1983…not just yet.

I was out of work having just graduated from Glendale Community College. In order to get back into the workforce, I needed to find a job. Normally, you looked at the want ads from the newspaper for jobs that you knew you could do.

Companies were looking for secretaries, which in today's world are now known as Administrative Assistants. These are fancy words for a low-paying job. Everybody needed a secretary, especially those trying to look important in the entertainment world.

The ad which I had been re-reading over and over that morning wasn't your typical secretarial want ad, which in itself was intriguing and made me grab the telephone and call the number listed at the bottom of the want ad.

Although the ad was vague, it appealed to me because I considered myself someone who was easygoing and liked to laugh. In fact, I considered myself an "easy laugh" which meant I tended to laugh at anything. Not that I was laughing like a hyena every day, but I loved a good joke, a double entendre phrase and a good punchline. The wit, the swiftness, and the unexpected punch at the end was perfection.

Late night television talk show host, Johnny Carson, was a master at it. As a child, I watched and studied the interaction between Johnny and the audience on *The Tonight Show* every night at 10:30 p.m., which was past my bedtime. Because my parents were so engrossed in the show, I managed to creep out of bed and hide from them. They always sat on the couch glued to the television set. They barely spoke to each other during the day, but yet they were sitting together busting a gut at the antics of a very young Johnny Carson with his guest star, Bob Hope.

All Johnny and Bob were doing was talking but they played off each other beautifully, trying to top one another, cracking up the audience and themselves.

Bob Hope was in rare form that night and I loved him.

"Have you heard about how the price of oil has gone up because of the crisis in the Middle East?" asked Bob. "I don't mind that the Arabs have us over a barrel, but I wish they'd be careful where they put that dipstick," said Bob.

Carson laughed up a storm.

Bob also quipped, "Whoever thought Oil of Olay would be the cheap stuff?"

My parents laughed so hard they were literally crying. For two people who hated each other, they were on the same page enjoying Bob Hope's jokes.

Bob made humorous observations on the world in general and about people and movie stars he thought were funny. The one-liners, the zings, and the jokes with punchlines that bounced around, were hilarious. Jokes were king like they had been back in the day of Vaudeville. Jokes that generated a laugh were highly prized.

BOB HOPE'S BUNGALOW: TALES FROM THE TYPING TRENCHES

As I mentioned before, Bob Hope had started out in Vaudeville in the 1920s and had a certain knack for the timing and delivery of the "joke." Looking back, I didn't think there was anybody funnier than Bob Hope.

That August morning, I thought to myself, could this job in the want ads possibly be for Bob Hope or Johnny Carson? Johnny Carson was doing his *Tonight Show* talk show at the NBC studios in Burbank which was next door to Glendale. So close, yet so far. It would be a miracle if I got a job working for Johnny. My imagination was in overdrive imagining how much fun it would be. I was so excited at the prospect.

I re-read the ad for the umpteenth time.

MUST HAVE SENSE OF HUMOR demanded the ad.

Rationalizing that demand, I knew I was an easy laugh, especially if the joke was funny.

Check sense of humor off the list. I definitely had one.

I reached for the telephone and dialed the number listed in the ad.

The phone on the other end of the line rang and rang and rang. Did I dial the right number, I wondered?

I was about to hang up when someone finally answered on the sixth ring.

"Apple One," said the receptionist.

I asked for the recruiter listed in the want ad.

Once the receptionist transferred me, the recruiter pummeled me with questions about my skills, where I had worked, the need for her to test me on the typewriter and then, and only then, could I get an interview. Just maybe.

I was a little annoyed that the recruiter was so curt and evasive when I asked her who the job was for. She told me it was for a man but very few of her clients had passed the interview stage. In fact, she doubted if I would be able to get past the front door. I think she got pleasure in knowing I would not pass *any* test.

I paused but held my tongue. It was as if the gauntlet was thrown down at my feet. Her comment made me more determined than ever to get the job.

"Come on in and take a typing test and we'll see what you've got," she told me with a snort.

What did I have to lose?

I drove over to the Apple One office and met with the recruiter.

My first impression of this woman was that she had a snarky look to her. She had a ferret face with a sneer which rivaled that of the famous late comic Jack Benny.

The recruiter probably thought the same of me because she gave me the once-over and rolled her eyes. We weren't subtle in our thoughts of each other.

I was set up at a typewriter with a preprinted yellow page of a typing sample staring at me.

"You have exactly five minutes to type this as fast as you can," she said and pushed down the black button on her stop watch.

I hurriedly rolled in a piece of paper into the typewriter cursing the fact that I was starting to sweat all the way down to my fingertips. I always hated being tested and this was no different.

Let me tell you, my fingers were flying across those keys on the typewriter lickety-split. As the timer ticked on and the recruiter glanced up at me, my head was bowed with a frown. I was concentrating so hard and my fingers were crashing down on the keys. I think I managed to chip a nail but continued on in a wild frenzy, ending in a concerto when the timer finally went "ding." Sweat poured down my back, my hands were shaking, but I had done it! I had typed the entire sheet that stood before me and more.

The recruiter strolled over to me and ripped out the paper from the typewriter with a smug look on her face. She knew no one could be accurate under the pressure of speed. She was certain that there would be hundreds of typing errors.

As she started to read my test paper, her smile began to fade. I cocked my head. Could I have typed a flawless typing test? I knew I was pretty good at typing, hitting speeds over 110 words per minute on a really good day.

The recruiter slapped my paper down on her desk. She didn't circle anything on the paper, just glared at me ferociously. I looked directly at her, a smirk was creeping over my lips. Take that you doubter of my typing excellence, I thought to myself.

Wiggling her index finger at me, the recruiter indicated she wanted me to come over to her desk. I got up and stood in front of her. She shoved a piece of paper at me.

"Take this address with you tomorrow. Be there at 9:00 a.m. sharp," she snarled at me.

I picked up the address from her desk.

"Who am I meeting?" I asked, waiting to hear the celebrity name.

"Nancy," she hissed, like everybody would know who Nancy was.

I stood there for a second, frowning at the address. Who the heck is Nancy, I thought as I stared at the recruiter.

The recruiter must have felt my eyes boring into her, because she lifted her hand and brushed her fingers at me in mid-air, shooing me away.

"That's all I can tell you," she said, like the job was a matter of national security.

She started dialing a phone number.

I looked around, then turned on my heel and walked away. I stopped at the door and looked back. The recruiter was on the phone smiling widely, obviously NOT speaking to a lowly job applicant on the other end.

I wondered what the heck I was getting into as I left the Apple One office.

Meet with the recruiter and get an interview. Check that off the list.

Tomorrow, crush the interview with "Nancy." In my mind, it was a checkmark already.

I had never met a celebrity in person, so Lord knows how I would react. Would I be dumbstruck, or would I just be friendly like I had known them for years? Normally, on business job interviews I always did the latter and got the job.

Last thing was to impress the celebrity. That was a possible checkmark in my mind.

Yes, I was about to go to an interview in Toluca Lake, to meet a Nancy, with no last name, and had no idea for whom I would be working. I felt like a secret agent on a mission.

I frowned and looked down at the Toluca Lake address. Toluca Lake was a very upper-class area near North Hollywood. One might even call it wealthy and quaint.

Jonathan Winters lived in that area, as well as singer Rick Springfield, and, of course, mega-comedian Bob Hope.

How bad could it be? I shrugged my shoulders. Shoot, this was exciting and I was game. The worst thing that could happen would be that I wouldn't get the job. The second worst thing would be if I DID get the job and the celebrity turned out to be a mean son of a gun. Some of my bosses have had a mean streak. I hate working for these mean people. Life's too short.

I always prided myself in doing research whenever I had to go into unknown territory. I had to do research on this address that I had in my hands. I liked to know who I would be working for in advance so I could tailor my interview skills to whatever the boss needed. What if it was a newsman or worse yet, a book author! What if it was a celebrity's attorney? I would be the one killing myself, if that was the case. Los Angeles attorneys were the toughest lawyers I had ever met. I remember one of them asking me to read back the dictation test and then challenging me that I had written down the wrong phrase. I stood my ground and told him that was exactly what he had said. Thank goodness the other attorney in the room agreed with me. Long story short, I was offered the job that afternoon. However, I turned it down flat because why work for someone who doesn't trust you at the get-go? That was the way I rolled. Trust me, and I'm yours. Challenge me, and I'm gone.

I was driving myself nuts trying to figure out who the celebrity was. What employment agency sends you on a job without telling you who you'd be working for? I decided I needed to scope out the address, and today! If the address was bogus, I still had time to back out of tomorrow's interview. I was a little cocky in those days.

Driving my green, souped-up 1974 Pontiac Firebird, the coolest car ever, I hopped on the 134 Freeway in Glendale and headed over to Burbank. I absolutely loved that car. It was so sexy and had power. Drivers would glance out their windows at my car and I could see how much they wished they had one.

I always had a lead foot when driving. So I hit the gas pedal and the car took flight. It was like the TV show, *The Dukes of Hazzard* (1979), only with a cooler green car.

I was anxious to check out the address in Toluca Lake. I hoped it was in a modern office building. Yeah, I was wrong once again.

As I got off the 134 Freeway, I cruised down the street to the address on Moorpark Street. I drove for quite a way without seeing any office buildings. I was confused. The area was lined with private and very expensive homes.

I looked at the map in my lap again and missed the building completely on my first drive by. Luckily, there were no cops about on Moorpark Street so I skidded to a stop and made a sweeping U-turn at the corner and drove back from where I had come as slowly as I possibly could. Drivers honked at me and ultimately passed by me with looks of "Why are you driving so slow, lady?" and other sweet terms of endearment, mainly used by truck drivers. People usually gave me the finger by yelling out their windows at me. The Burbank drivers restrained themselves which was a pleasant surprise to me.

Then I noticed the small plaque of numbers on the brick wall that surrounded the home. It read 10346. I had found it! The place was hidden behind a huge brick wall covered with ivy which went on for the entire block. I couldn't see anything but a small driveway leading into the compound. So much for reconnaissance unless I wanted to stop and scale the wall and look over. I might have done so but there wasn't any parking on Moorpark Street so I just drove to the corner and pulled over.

What was I getting myself into, I wondered? This was crazy. I could get behind that wall and be murdered! No one would ever know. The recruiter didn't give a damn. I could be a dead woman, wiped off the face of the map by an unnamed celebrity wielding a weapon. I was already a little afraid about an unsolved stalker murder case in the Glendale area which was on the news. Now I had convinced myself that I could be walking into a trap with a celebrity killer. The house was in an exclusive suburb near North Hollywood, but still! I sat at the corner for a second and gathered my thoughts.

My mind was churning, but the thrill of the meeting was too weird to pass up. I had to know who the celebrity was. I was going to that interview tomorrow, come hell or high water! Little did I know that I was in for the adventure of a lifetime!

Chapter 3

THE INTERVIEW

The employment recruiter never told me who I was going to work for in Toluca Lake until the day of the interview. It was all cloak and dagger and kind of exciting to me in a weird way.

Finally, the day had arrived to officially go to the address in Toluca Lake. I still wasn't sure who the celebrity was. All I understood was that the celebrity needed someone with a sense of humor. I knew TV comedian Jonathan Winters lived in Toluca Lake as well as singer Rick Springfield who was famous for his song "Jessie's Girl." I had also heard that Bob Hope lived somewhere in the area. But never in my dreams would I have suspected what was soon to happen.

When I went to the secret address, the Office Manager, Nancy, met with me and asked about my background. As I gave her the highlights of my legal background working for lawyers, I kept trying to pull at my bushy, frizzy hair to make it lie down. Nothing worked. As soon as I lifted my hand from my head, the end I was holding down would pop up again with gusto. It was a losing battle. I looked like Janis Joplin on speed, but I didn't care anymore. Forget the hair! Forget Janis! Forget it all!

Nancy ignored my plight with the hair and said the job was for Bob Hope as a second secretary. The big question was, did I like dogs. You bet I did. Actually, I loved all animals. The next test then was to have one of the dogs come in and sniff my hand. No sudden movements, she warned as Snowjob walked over to me. He smelled my hand and even licked my fingers. I stroked his white fur, rubbed his tummy, and gave him air kisses until we finally bonded. Man, six hours never whizzed by so quickly. Snowjob wouldn't leave me alone. I had to throw a ball for him over and over and over. This went on for quite a while because Nancy actually got up and made a cup of tea. Guess I made a favorable impression because Nancy thought I would also get along with Lead Secretary # 1, Kathy.

I only hoped I wouldn't have to throw a ball for her as well.

Finally, Nancy offered me the job as Secretary # 2 and I was to start the next day. I made the staggering sum of $330 a week before taxes. Yes, the money was low, but the job was great. I literally laughed every single day.

Everyone knew that Bob loved jokes about politics and entertainment. One Bob Hope joke in particular I really liked. It goes something like this: "California's back to a two-party system: the Democrats and the Screen Actors Guild." That was funny stuff. Now I ask you, what office can you work at and hear laughs like those every day?

Truth be told, I was thrilled to get the job and scared all at once. I was going to enter the world of Bob Hope! Oh boy! Breathe, just breathe!

Nancy left me with a few words before I departed. Secretary # 1, Kathy, was older and easygoing but she didn't want anyone too flashy to outshine her, so stay in my lane.

My hair actually sealed the deal. How could I outshine Kathy? I had a full head of clown hair for God's sake!

BOB HOPE'S BUNGALOW: Tales From The Typing Trenches

After the interview with Nancy, I stopped at Marie Callender's Restaurant and called the employment agency to give them the good word. At first the recruiter thought I was pulling her leg. As we were talking, she simultaneously got a call from Mr. Hope's Office Manager asking that they send over the paperwork. They had hired me! To say that the recruiter was flabbergasted was an understatement. She was dumbstruck. She never expected Miss Brillo Pad head would get the job.

When I got back to the employment agency, the recruiter was all smiles and pats on the back. There were lots of congratulations and "we knew you could do it" comments from everyone. The recruiter had pulled out a year's worth of supplies with the company name emblazoned on them.

I was loaded down with all sorts of pens, pads, cups, anything with the employment agency's name on it, to bring over to Bob Hope's on my first day. I thought it was crass but I brought everything with me anyway.

When I showed the marketing trinkets to Nancy, she agreed with me that they were junk, and we threw everything out on my first day.

Chapter 4

ENTER LAUGHING

My whole world changed after I went to that Toluca Lake interview. The air smelled fresher, food tasted better, and I was actually excited.

For my first day, I wanted to be early so I would look conscientious. The fastest route was by freeway. I hopped on the 134 Freeway, and headed west, lead footing it all the way in my beautiful key lime green 1974 Firebird.

I clicked on the radio and heard Michael Jackson's "Wanna Be Startin' Somethin'." I turned it up, way up, to full blast.

When I pulled off the freeway in Burbank I noticed in my rearview mirror a California Highway Patrol officer was behind me. Could it be because I was speeding? No! Not today! But yes, he pulled me over and I sat in my car humiliated as car after car on the street passed by me. People were gawking. I tried the old standby of tears. That didn't work. Probably he was put off by my bushy hair.

BOB HOPE'S BUNGALOW: Tales From The Typing Trenches

Let me just say that this was the unkind era of Big Hair. Big, fat, permed hair. Hair that could receive messages from aliens in outer space. Yes, it was that big. Weird, dry, curly, full of static, awful hair! Yikes! I looked like a cartoon character after I got out of the salon. I had never had a perm in my life, and what resulted was atrocious! My hair was so fried and stuck out like I had put my finger into an electric wall plug and got electrocuted. And that hair never ever went down, no matter how much water or oil I plastered on it. And hairspray? Forget about it! My hair was curly beyond belief. Imagine Little Orphan Annie in a short skirt and high heels and you'll understand my panic when I had to report to the new job with that hair! I was doomed.

Good grief, whoever thought perms were attractive? I'd like to smack him upside the head because undoubtedly it was a man!

The cop wrote the ticket, I signed it and he handed it back to me.

He said, "Slow down and, oh, have a nice day, ma'am."

Ma'am? Why do cops do that? As soon as they give you a ticket, you know darn well that your day is in shambles. No niceness would be happening that day. It's kind of a revenge thing with cops, I think. You can't talk them out of a ticket and they know it. They have to make their quota of tickets and I always ended up with the short stick. Maybe because I *was* short?

I tried to adjust my clown hair but it was not having it. I still looked like a bomb had gone off in my hair. The only thing was to take a deep breath and shrug off the ticket. I was not going to let this tiny driving blunder affect my first day on the job. I'll make lemons out of lemonade. Or was it the other way?

I drove over to West Riverside Drive, turned left on Foreman Avenue, and then cut over to Moorpark Street on the right. I quickly found the ivy wall on the left along Moorpark and the driveway leading into the private home.

My green 1974 Firebird edged carefully up the driveway. I parked my car outside of the Bungalow. There was a huge electric gate farther down the driveway which you had to be buzzed into by a security guard. The wide gate was attached to the ivy wall all the way to the Bungalow. I got out and walked over to the entrance. I stood on the step next to the double Dutch door and knocked. I waited for someone to let me in.

I was nervous. I was scared. I had no idea what I was getting into. I liked jokes and comedians but had no idea how crazy it could get or how much fun it would be. I was a wreck.

I knew I was early when I knocked on the double Dutch door. I heard someone unlock several locks to the double Dutch door. It felt like I was entering a prison. Locks were turning, gears were clicking. I had my hands in my pockets and crumpled the speeding ticket in my hand. Finally, the door creaked open like a crypt.

It was Marie, the tall blonde who worked for Nancy, the Office Manager.

"Sorry, these locks are sometimes hard to turn," she said.

"Guess they are made to keep out the riffraff," I said. She didn't react. Bad joke. Why did I say it? I'm not a gag writer. Funny wasn't in my DNA. Man, this was going to be a tough day, I thought to myself.

Fortunately, Marie tossed a quick smile at me and pushed open the door to let me in.

She mumbled something else as I stepped inside.

Did I hear her right? Did she just say, "Welcome to the nut house?" Nut, as in crazy?

I must have not heard her right. Or did I? I shook my head. I was just nervous, I told myself. First the ticket, then the bad joke. What's next? What could possibly be next?

Nancy had just hung up from her phone call and got up and came over to me as I stepped inside.

"Welcome," she said, smiling at me. I noticed she glanced at my hair.

We did the usual shaking of hands.

"Marie will show you around. I've got to take care of something for Mrs. Hope," said Nancy and went back to her desk.

And so my first day had begun.

I was officially inside the prison, I mean, the nut house, according to Marie.

BOB HOPE'S BUNGALOW: TALES FROM THE TYPING TRENCHES

I still had time to make a break for it, but I suppressed that urge.

Sometimes you just have to go with it.

Marie was friendly and nice and didn't say a word about my hair. That was a good sign. If Marie and Nancy were willing to ignore it, I was going to ignore it, too.

Marie showed me to my desk which was a metal army desk at the back of the large room.

It was the former secretary's desk. This secretary had been "wounded" on the job. Of course, I knew nothing of what had happened. They kept that a closely-guarded secret. What employer in his right mind would tell you, "Welcome aboard but don't ever go outside and watch out for the man-eating dogs. They are trained guard dogs with an attitude. If you blink at them wrong, they'll rip your face off."

Yes, the last secretary was indeed taken out by one of the guard dogs. Hey, it's not every day you get eaten by the family pet!

Marie told me Kathy was the Head Secretary # 1 and she would be in the office at 10 a.m. Kathy sat in an exact replica of my metal army desk to the right of my desk. My old typewriter faced the bookkeeper's office. Kathy faced the vault when she was typing. There was a supply room directly in front of me. Actually, my desk was straddling the supply room and the hallway leading up toward Nancy's and Marie's desks. Windows were behind me overlooking the lush large back yard and in the middle of all of this was a wall of old-time photos. There were pictures of old churches, old men with big mustaches, and a map of old Italy from the 1930s. Everything was old and wrinkled, including a picture of Bob Hope. Things smelled a little musty which I wrote off as either Nancy's or Marie's perfume. What did I know?

I was officially the youngest woman in the office. Apparently, Dolores, the wife of Mr. Hope, did not allow any woman to work there if she was less than thirty years old and pretty. Emphasis on pretty. Phew, I just made it in. I'm not sure about the "pretty" rule, so I must have looked ugly enough due to my recent perm. Nothing makes you look god-awful than a bad perm. I guess Dolores Hope thought I was old and ugly. I didn't care. It was a nearby job, in the entertainment industry, and most importantly, I needed the money.

As I got the lay of the land that first day, Nancy and Marie gave me the lists of writers and the combinations to the two vaults.

Nancy also mentioned that Mrs. Hope insisted that the secretaries address Bob as "Mr. Hope" at all times. That way, everyone knew their place. Mr. and Mrs. Hope were the royalty and the rest of us were the help. You know, like in the TV show *Upstairs Downstairs*. It didn't bother me since I came from the wrong side of the tracks anyway.

Marie went out of her way to help me in any way that she could. She was one of those people you immediately liked. She always had words of wisdom to offer which I wished I had written down. That morning I tried not to get too close to Marie as we walked through the office, because one quick turn of my head, and she'd be knocked to the floor by my big hair. Yes, my hair was that lethal. I probably should have got arrested for wearing that big, permed helmet-head hairdo. It was dry, brittle, big, and most of all, BAD! Worse than bad! It was god-awful! The women of that era must have all drunk the Kool-Aid because we sported those perm jobs like a badge of courage. What were we thinking, was all I could ask myself as I tried to straighten out one of those big ass curls with my saliva by holding my hand over it, to no avail. When I removed my hand, the curl bounced back to attention and just stood out like a giant curly onion ring!

Nancy got a call from Dolores Hope, Bob's wife, and hurriedly rushed off with her steno pad under her arm to assist Mrs. Hope in the main house.

"What's in the vaults?" I casually asked Marie who was looking at my hair. I thought she was going to do that monkey thing, where one dominant monkey starts parting the other's hair for bugs, or was it dandruff? I never could remember what their mission was.

Marie looked me in the eye and smiled.

"Those are the jokes from the last fifty-plus years," said Marie nonchalantly.

"A vault of old jokes? Is the paper still intact after fifty years?" I asked.

BOB HOPE'S BUNGALOW: TALES FROM THE TYPING TRENCHES

"Of course. Mr. Hope used to write his own jokes but over the years everyone who was funny wrote for him," replied Marie.

"So, he's got them in a vault in case there's a fire?" I asked.

"Mainly, the vault was to deter anyone from trying to steal them," said Marie.

"Who would want to steal old jokes?" I asked with a smile, thinking I was funny.

"You'd be surprised," she said and sauntered back to her desk in the front.

I watched her. Marie was very tall. Compared to her I was a shrimp. I stood about five-foot-three inches and she must have been closer to five-foot-ten. Actually, with her full blonde hair, she seemed a lot taller. Golly, I would have killed to be five-foot-ten. Maybe short people are just funnier because they are short of stature and use their wit to look smarter and, in turn, taller. Don't quote me. It's just a theory of mine.

When Marie went back to her desk, I was curious about the vault in the wall. It was the size of a door. I stood in front of the larger vault and spun the black dial of tiny little numbers. It made a ticking sound as it spun around. When it stopped, I lined up a number from the secret combination Marie had given me. The line on the dial had to match the center of the number. Then I had to move the dial backwards to get to the second secret number. There were four more numbers to line up perfectly. Then you had to use a large lever to push down on and *Voila!*, the door would swing open.

Inside the black vault there were lots and lots of file cabinets lined up in a row. It was a giant filing room, I thought. The other vault was exactly the same. I peeked inside the files and saw jokes for every show Bob Hope had ever performed, dating back decades. It was kind of a mystical experience for me seeing the famous Bob Hope jokes throughout the century. I felt like crossing myself and genuflecting. But that soon passed because my phone on my desk was ringing.

I ran out of the file room and was about to pick up the receiver, then I froze. What was I supposed to say? Bob Hope's office? Mr. Hope's residence? The phone kept ringing.

Nervously, I called out to Marie who was in the front: "Do I say Bob Hope's office or residence?"

"Just say hello," she replied simply.

I raised my eyebrows and said to myself, just hello? Well, any idiot can do that and I fit the profile.

According to Marie, my primary job was to type up all of the jokes from the writers and get them to Mr. Hope. Jokes were usually due every day from the writers on staff. I was looking forward to everyone calling in to tell me jokes. Sounded easy enough. I was an excellent stenographer. I could write down anything verbatim at 120 words per minute using my Gregg shorthand.

The phone was still ringing.

I sat down in the chair with a loud squeaky plop and answered the phone with a deep-throated Marilyn Monroe voice, "Hello." It sure didn't sound like me. I'm usually a medium kind of voice. Go figure why I chose to speak like Marilyn Monroe.

"Who's this?" asked the caller on the other end of the line. He, too, was confused.

"I'm Carol. And you are…" I queried still in my deep throat. God, I sounded like a man.

"Robert Mills. One of the writers. Oh, wait a minute, you're Bob's new secretary, right?" he asked.

"That's me," I said with a grin. My Marilyn Monroe moment was gone. Everybody finds me out sooner or later. And it was usually sooner.

"Welcome aboard! And relax, it's going to be a fun ride," he laughed.

Oh sure, I thought, a clown-haired, deep-throated shrimp was about to start work for the famous, world-renowned Bob Hope. I was so nervous, thinking I'd be run out of town on a rail. I wasn't sure rails were legal to put you on, but I did know I was extremely nervous. I could feel sweat beginning to roll down my armpits. You know it always starts small, but by the end of the day, you look like you've been through a car wash.

I let out a deep, shaky breath, then shook my fingers, trying to relax.

And fun? I had never worked for a celebrity, let alone the world's most famous comedian.

All I really wanted to do in that moment was throw up.

"So how many writers are there?" I asked.

"Ten, maybe more," Robert said.

I gulped. My eyes widened. That's why there were two vaults of jokes!

"Let's get started, shall we?" he said.

Robert started to recite his first joke and I wrote it down verbatim using my shorthand. Before he got to the end of the joke, Robert stopped talking.

"Are you getting this?" he asked worriedly.

"Yes, sir," I said.

"I don't hear a typewriter," he said suspiciously.

"Oh, well that's because I'm taking it down in shorthand," I replied with great confidence.

"No, no, no, no, no! You can't do that! You've got to TYPE the jokes exactly as I say them! Verbatim. Put some paper into the typewriter and let's start again," he said.

I raised my eyebrows and screwed up my face as I rolled a sheet of paper into the electric typewriter. I didn't like this guy telling me what to do. I was a professional secretary! I knew what to do! It was my job.

"Ready?" he asked.

"As I'll ever be," I said, poised to type, my fingers in the air. Talk about old school, I thought.

He dictated and I typed.

He said, "You got that?"

"Yep," I said.

"Okay, good. It's not that I don't trust you, but read the joke back to me."

I rolled my eyes. Robert doesn't trust me. I rolled the typed paper toward me. Then I read back the joke perfectly, word for word. It was cute and I smiled.

Robert was satisfied and we continued on. Next joke.

He had about twenty jokes. The more he read, the funnier they got and I tried not to laugh. By the end of his reading, I thought all the jokes were hilarious. Mostly, I bit my lip to control my laughing urge.

"Now all you have to do is make a copy of them and get the jokes up to Bob Hope," said Robert.

He was a good teacher. Strict, but good. And funny. I'd give Robert a solid "A."

We hung up and I started to make a copy of Robert's jokes.

Just then another call came in. This call was from the head writer, Gene Perret. The top dog! Oh my goodness, I thought, Gene was the big cheese of writers! I was so nervous.

I have to say Gene Perret was my favorite head writer so far. He was even keel and basically all around adorable. He was just about the sweetest man, so quiet, yet hilarious. He wrote the book on how to write comedy. Gene had been in comedy since the early 1960s writing for Phyllis Diller and Slappy White. Gene wrote for *Laugh-In* (1968) and won three Emmys as a staff writer for *The Carol Burnett Show* (1967). With his resume, how could Bob Hope go wrong?

After the Robert episode, Gene really caught me off guard. He was so soft spoken and in a very good mood. There was a little "good to have you on board" and "you're going to love this job," before we buckled down to work.

I sat in front of the typewriter and did as before, typing up each joke exactly as Gene Perret read them to me.

Gene didn't challenge me or ask me to read back any of his jokes. He was so easygoing and said he would call later in the afternoon because he had a conference call with Mr. Hope.

I now had forty jokes that I had to copy and bring to Mr. Hope. I was about to gather up all of the jokes, when the phone rang for the third time.

I looked at the clock. It wasn't 9:15 a.m. yet. Jeepers, how many more calls could I take, I wondered.

I picked up the phone with my usual husky "Hello."

BOB HOPE'S BUNGALOW: Tales From The Typing Trenches

This time it was Phillip Jayson Lasker, another staff writer. But this call I felt was a tad different.

Phil was a young writer who was very nice and polite to boot. He sounded younger than the first two callers. Maybe thirty years old? I couldn't tell a man's age by his phone voice.

I believe Phillip Jayson Lasker was one of the youngest male joke writers on staff at the time. The reason I'm singling him out was because he was an absolute riot. Don't get me wrong. The other staff writers were just as funny but Phil was special. He was funny, yet unassuming, and he laughed with me whenever I started laughing. He was kind of goofy and had this "yuk yuk" laugh. It was infectious. He made me laugh whenever he started with his yuk yuks. I actually found him endearing. I knew he was married, but I couldn't help myself. He was kind of cute and charming and sweet, and had this great wit. I loved his jokes that he called in daily for me to type up and deliver to Mr. Hope. I would giggle at every turn of a phrase and chortle out loud at the punchline.

I laughed so heartily that I disturbed Frances, the bookkeeper, in the other room. She always had her door open facing my desk. Truth be told, I developed a mini-crush on Phil. Then again, maybe it was his humor that I was attracted to. I'm not sure. If he had been single, with a capital "S," I would have made a move on him. Luckily, he never had to find out. Phew! Flirting with men is no easy feat. I sort of tried to flirt, or I was outright flirting, I don't remember. But it was fun and I think it was fun for them, too. At least I hoped it was. How boring an office would be without the occasional flirt.

Quite frankly, I laughed at all the writers' jokes. I couldn't help it. The jokes were so darn funny! And I typed them up every single day. There's nothing like the smell of laughter first thing in the morning!

God bless the writers. They could be anywhere, and come up with twenty sure fire side-splitting jokes. When I say twenty, I mean twenty per writer. That was minimum. Multiply the twenty jokes times nine or ten writers. Mr. Hope at eighty years of age had plenty of material but he wanted more! Fresh jokes of the times. Topics were handed down each morning to the staff writers and, by God, there were hundreds of jokes every day presented to Mr. Hope to pick and choose from. I can see why Servicemen loved these jokes so much. It takes a special mind to spin a quick-witted one or two liner into a loaded punchline that came as a surprise at the end and a delight. The writers had special minds indeed. They were either special or demented. I haven't figured out which. Let's just go with funny, because I laughed at them all. Sometimes I even knew the punchline that was coming. I had written my own share of funny lines in a *Cheers* spec script and a *Who's the Boss* spec script, so I am familiar with funny. In addition, I was an avid sitcom viewer.

As I was saying, Phil had another twenty jokes which were all on the same topic of the day.

I started to type but there was something in Phil's delivery of the jokes that started me giggling. By now, I had heard forty jokes. When Phil started reading off his batch, my laugh meter went into overdrive. I was almost punch drunk with jokes! I couldn't contain my laughter. I could hear Phil on the other end of the line laughing along with me. That made me giggle all the more. And you know what happens when one person starts to go, right? So does the other.

Then the laugh that came out of Phil was so unexpectedly funny, it caught me by surprise. It was a drawn-out, gasping for air "yuk." That's all I needed. I was already cooked on both sides by just the jokes.

With Phil's drawn-out "yuk," and a second one added for good measure, I laughed even harder. He started with an intake of air. Then I heard the "yuk" from Phil. Then he sucked in more air, another "yuk," more air, and another "yuk" which was stretched out. It's hard to explain. Who couldn't laugh at that sound? The more Phil did it, the harder I laughed. Actually, it was involuntary laughing on my part. I really didn't want to laugh this hysterically. I was literally crying because the sounds of "yuk, yuk, yuk" were teetering on the edge of the Roadrunner's sound effects of zip, bam, whoosh, and in the next frame, the Roadrunner is off down the road in a cloud of dust. I always laughed at the Roadrunner and so did everyone else.

Tears came out of my eyes and streamed down my face as I listened to Phil go on. Both of us laughed and laughed. I'm sure he thought I was laughing at the joke. But the jokes, coupled with the yuk yuks were just too much. Granted, I'm an easy laugh, but this whole scene just put me over the edge. It was ridiculous. I was certifiably hysterical! I guess it was part stress of a new job, the yuk yuk sound effects, and the non-stop giggling.

I was laughing, crying, and trying to clear my throat all at the same time. My head was lying on my desk. I was like a huge marlin on the desk, flopping around, quivering with laughter.

At that moment, Kathy, the Head Secretary # 1, came into the office and found me in that state of quivering, crying, and holding my stomach, still on the phone, but unable to stop laughing, or catch my breath. I looked over at her, unable to form a word, just crying with laughter.

She saw the scene and just smiled. Apparently, she had been through it, too.

"Typing up the jokes, I see," she grinned and sat down at the desk nearer to the vault.

I couldn't breathe, I couldn't talk, and my side was killing me. I tried to pull myself together and let Phil continue dictating his other jokes to me, all the while under the watchful eye of Frances, the bookkeeper, who glared at me from the next room. She didn't appreciate why I almost wet my pants.

That's how my first day began and every day thereafter. Jokes upon jokes, by the best in the business. I couldn't stop laughing and walked around all day with a smile on my face. My side hurt, but it was worth it.

What a great dream job, I thought to myself! Who gets to go to work and laugh every single day? Could I *be* any luckier?

Chapter 5

1983, ME, AND THE WILD WEST

To give you a sense of 1983, the important news of the day included the Strategic Defense Initiative, also known as Star Wars, Harrods bombing by the IRA in London, the Space Shuttle Challenger launching, the worst drought and famine in history in Ethiopia resulting in 4 million dead, the first mobile phones were introduced to the public by Motorola, and the United States deployed cruise missiles in Europe. It was also the year the Internet was created and Microsoft Word was launched.

1983 was the year the United States invaded Grenada.

Sally Ride's first flight aboard the Space Shuttle Challenger made her the first American woman in space.

Margaret Thatcher became Prime Minister of England.

The last episode of *M*A*S*H* (1972) finally aired on television in 1983 with 125 million viewers. A fun bit of trivia was the Korean War only lasted three years (1950-1953) as compared to eleven television seasons of the series.

BOB HOPE'S BUNGALOW: TALES FROM THE TYPING TRENCHES

Cabbage Patch dolls were extremely popular and sold in shops.

The top films of the day in 1983 included: *Tootsie, Trading Places, WarGames, Flashdance, Staying Alive, Terms of Endearment,* and *Yentl.*

The popular musicians were: Phil Collins, The Police, David Bowie, Culture Club, Duran Duran, Elton John, Pink Floyd, Ozzy Osbourne, Rod Stewart, and The Moody Blues. Michael Jackson and Lionel Ritchie also topped the music charts.

The average cost of rent per month was $335.

Gas was 96 cents a gallon.

The yearly income was around $21,070. Imagine living on that today!

The Night Stalker, Richard Ramirez, was on the loose and killing people in Glendale where I, unfortunately, ran into him at a bar one night.

Glendale Fire Captain John Orr was also sneaking around setting fires in Glendale and Pasadena.

It was, indeed, a year of many changes whether we were ready for them or not.

And I wasn't.

In the eighties people left a message on your home answering machine if you were out of the house. Many a time I came home to a red blinking light on my answering machine only to find I had five messages which turned out to be either hang-ups or someone breathing heavily into the receiver. No message. Just heavy breathing. The first one I heard was a real turn on. I had never been exposed to such baseness in my life. Who gets a kick out of breathing into a phone like they've got asthma? California always had its share of nuts, and I admit I dated a couple of them in the 1980s.

Most people described me as the girl next door. I stood five-foot-three inches tall. My weight was about one hundred pounds soaking wet. In those days I had curly big hair with red highlights, and a very trim figure. The only things I didn't have were big breasts. I cannot tell you how many times I lamented about that! I made up for it by wearing the shortest skirts and dresses I could find. Legs sometimes got you noticed. And I wasn't scared to show them. My dark silky nylons added to the appeal. I knew how to walk because my flirtatious British mother taught me. Mum said to wiggle as you walk and stand up straight, for God's sake! Years of hearing those exact words did the trick for me. I stood up straight, mainly because I wanted to be taller. I would have killed to be five inches taller!

Naturally, I flirted with all the men I met, and usually they responded in kind. There was a fifty-fifty chance that I'd meet the man of my dreams, I thought. Actually, I really wasn't looking for a long-term commitment. I wanted to have fun, just like in the Cyndi Lauper song, "Girls Just Want to Have Fun." If you can't have fun in Los Angeles, where can you?

I wore the latest fashions and was very stylish. Another thing my mother taught me. Short skirts were still in vogue, hot pants, and psychedelic colors were now old school in the 1980s, but I still loved them. The tighter, the shorter, the better was my motto.

My favorite sports were skating, skiing, and ice hockey which were old holdovers from my youth in Canada. Dance also filled my life. I learned ballet dancing at an early age. While dancing on a stage in front of hundreds of people was out of my comfort zone, I pushed through and excelled at it. That was how I rolled. Show me a challenge and I'll conquer it.

I also loved the movies and spent hours at the cinema watching the classics. Later, I penned a few spec screenplays which never went anywhere. But one can always dream, right?

The music of the 1980s pumped through my veins and I loved everything from hard rock to psychedelic to even the Bee Gees. In the early eighties the music rocked to a different beat. Michael Jackson's song "Billy Jean" was cruising up the charts, and The Police had a huge hit with their song, "Every Little Thing She Does Is Magic."

When my girlfriends and I went out to a night club, we took over the place. If a great song was playing and no one would be out on the dance floor, I got up and danced with myself. That's when the men started to take notice. Whenever I was rocking out on the dance floor, sure enough, a guy would come over and start to dance with me. I could dance all night long without getting tired. I was wired and wasn't afraid to shake my booty with any man, woman, or alien from outer space who cared to join in. I wasn't picky. I just wanted to dance!

I trained to be a ballerina when I was very young. When I heard the latest music on the radio, it was so hip and cool. I even tried to practice my ballet movements to it. That proved to be a problem with toe shoes. In my early twenties, I would dance for hours in my apartment with the stereo blaring. I absolutely lived for the beat of the music. Usually, the neighbors would pound on the walls, but I felt electrified and just wanted to bust out! Music can be so liberating.

I remember my friends and I checking out the music scene at the clubs in West Hollywood and Beverly Hills. Men were available and everywhere. It was music, sex, and rock and roll, which was only the best combination ever!

One night my girlfriends and I walked into a building that had a giant dance floor upon entering. Guys were standing along the two sides of the room checking out the girls as they entered the club. A couple of them walked up to me and started asking questions. Do you come here often? Can I buy you a drink? The last question from this guy was the winning question. We sat down with him and his buddies for quite a while. Liquor was flowing and we were all getting a little drunk. The place was packed. There were lots of dancers on the floor. At the tables, quite a few recreational drugs were passed around. At this time, in the 1980s, marijuana was not legal in California. It didn't matter though. Everyone had it and shared it. I tried my best to get high but never could. I would inhale, as opposed to Clinton, but nothing happened. I was bummed because all my friends were buzzed. My Canadian constitution was stronger than I thought. Alcohol was the only drug that worked for me.

After the club closed down for the night, all the girls and guys went out to breakfast where everyone exchanged phone numbers. This ritual was always the same every weekend, only with different players. It was a fun way to meet new people.

A lot of these young guys that we met were aspiring actors, musicians, and writers. That was quite a change from the Minnesota boys where I came from. Most of the Minnesotans were up-and-coming bankers, lawyers, and techie types. They were the same fun guys but with different goals.

I was too young to date in Canada, where there were a lot of nationalities from French, and English to Native North American Indians living in provincial Manitoba.

I thought California was the Wild West. Anything could and did happen in Los Angeles.

The Sharon Tate murders by the Manson family were still on my mind, even years later, so I didn't take too many chances with dating strangers.

Serial killer Ted Bundy was active in the late 1970s.

Actor Sal Mineo was stabbed to death on the Los Angeles streets.

In 1980, Playmate Dorothy Stratten was shot to death by her estranged husband. You might say murder was not a stranger to those who lived in Los Angeles.

My apartment was in the suburb of Glendale, sandwiched between Burbank and Eagle Rock. Later I heard that the infamous serial killer Richard Ramirez had also lived nearby.

The newspapers reported that in 1984 Ramirez had killed a woman in Glassell Park which was just south of Forest Lawn in Glendale. It was very close to my apartment.

Dubbed the Night Stalker, Ramirez also killed two other residents of Glendale the following year.

As you can see, death was swirling all around me, but I was oblivious to it. Usually, my friends and I traveled in packs just for safety reasons. Although I drove by those sad places all the time, I never gave it a second thought. It's funny that the youth think they are invincible, isn't it? We will all die someday, so I say, enjoy the ride while you can.

Chapter 6

THE WRITERS

There were eight men and one woman on staff. The male staff writers included Gene Perret, Robert Mills, Freddy Fox, Mort Lachman, Seaman Jacobs, Doug Gamble, Tom Shadyac, and Phillip Jayson Lasker. There was also Bob Hope's first female staff writer, Martha Bolton. Kathy Green wasn't on staff but she contributed part time to the joke telling. She said she'd do it for free because she loved Mr. Hope. Who didn't?

Of course I had the other list of writers that Nancy gave to me. It was a Who's Who of some of the finest minds in comedy: There was also Mel Frank, Marshall Flaum, Hal Kanter, and Mel Shavelson. Larry Gelbart, Pat Proft, Sherwood Schwartz, and Gig Henry were all before my time.

The writers were funny and fast at coming up with jokes which was important to Bob.

In fact, in the event of a nuclear explosion, Mr. Hope kept his own emergency supply of food, water, and four or five writers on tap in the bowels of the Bungalow.

I started to get good at the rhythm of jokes and after a while I could almost come up with the punchline before the writer dictated it to me.

It was so automatic that I listened for the punchline and laughed out loud when it came. I was, in essence, the first audience reaction to a writer's joke. The writers always appreciated my laughter because I didn't just titter a little. Oh no, it was bust-a-gut, full-body laughter. For over a year, my job was to type the jokes and woe was me if I didn't laugh at each and every one of them. It was an unspoken law that I laugh at the jokes. If I didn't, I can assure you, the writers would get a little insecure. When I didn't laugh at all, I soon found the writers asking me to toss out their joke altogether. God forbid the joke wasn't funny! I would have been run out of town on a rail. But the jokes were always funny, come rain or shine. Thousands of jokes to revel in and that is exactly what I did. I absolutely loved a good joke. I guess you could call me the judge of the joke. No, that was not true, because only Bob Hope could judge a joke, having spent sixty-plus years telling them to audiences all over the world. That was why Bob Hope was the King of Comedy. I typed the jokes and laughed my head off after each and every joke. Typing jokes was my favorite job in the whole world! I was told I should have been a professional audience member because my laughter was so infectious to everyone, except for the bookkeeper, Frances.

I couldn't blame her. Frances was drowning in dull numbers all day long.

On the other hand, I felt like I was lying on an inflatable raft in a swanky swimming pool holding a martini glass teaming with jokes!

Chapter 7

THE HOPE FAMILY

Before I go any further discussing Bob Hope, let me introduce you to the Hope family.

Dolores Hope

I rarely saw Bob's wife, Mrs. Dolores Hope. She interacted with Nancy every day. She had a separate life from Bob Hope. She did her own thing from going with her sister to meet the Pope in Vatican City to lunching with the girls.

I do remember one day when Bob Hope asked me to come upstairs to his office that while Mr. Hope was rifling through a desk for something, Mrs. Hope was outside in an interior hallway knocking on the door.

I waited for Mr. Hope to open the door for her. He either didn't hear her or was just ignoring her. She stood in that hallway and the pounding got louder and louder. It felt like a 5.0 earthquake. Mr. Hope finally went to the door and said I could go. As I was leaving through the other door, Bob opened the door to his wife, just as I shut my door and walked down the steps to the driveway.

However, there was one thing Mrs. Hope made very clear. Any attractive woman on staff was to be above reproach in her interactions with Mr. Hope. I thought both Nancy and Marie were quite attractive, but then again, they worked for Mr. Hope's wife. I had this frizzy permed hair, so I was out of the attractive category. Kathy was a mature woman with wisps of grey in her hair and very professional. Actually, there weren't any attractive women on Mr. Hope's secretarial staff to worry about.

I'm surprised she let Marie and Nancy in, but then again I think they were off limits since they were married to terrific guys. That's my theory and I'm sticking with it.

Bob and Dolores Hope had a total of four adopted children: Linda, Tony, Kelly and Nora. All the Hope children were grown with lives of their own when I came on the scene.

Nora Hope

Eleanora, also known as Nora, Hope was born in 1930 and adopted by the Hopes in 1946.

Linda Hope

Linda Hope was Bob and Dolores Hope's second oldest adopted child born in 1933 and adopted in 1939.

Linda lived just across the street from the Hope house and came over once in a blue moon. She was friendly and always had a smile on her face. I remember her coming through the Bungalow and saying "hi." Then off she went into the main house to see her parents. I didn't see her again for another week or so.

Kelly Hope

Kelly was the adopted son of Bob and Dolores. He was born in 1937 and adopted in 1946. He was never around during the year I served.

Tony Hope

Anthony, also known as Tony, was born and adopted in 1940 and became a Washington attorney and lobbyist. He died in 2004.

Chapter 8

MY FIRST MEETING WITH BOB HOPE

The first time I met Bob Hope was when he called my desk phone and said he needed me to come up to his room.

"I'll be right there," I said into the phone but he had hung up by that time.

This would be my first time meeting Bob Hope in the flesh. I gathered up my notebook and pen and dashed out of the small staff Bungalow and into the courtyard which led up to the main house. I was literally running like I was being timed and could not be late. What a sight for sore eyes that was.

Mr. Hope's room could be reached on the outside of his two-story mansion by going up the stairs to his room which overlooked the driveway. I ran up the stairs, tripping on the second step, and when I finally got to the top, I knocked on Bob Hope's big door.

BOB HOPE'S BUNGALOW: TALES FROM THE TYPING TRENCHES

A man that I didn't know answered the door.

As he flung the door open, I saw he was big, tall, dark and handsome and dressed impeccably. Was he Italian? *Mama Mia*, he was cute, even if he did have short-cropped hair as compared to the long-haired guys I dated. Was he the agent for Mr. Hope, I wondered as I drank him in with my eyes? I hoped he was Mark Anthony. Aren't all agents sexy with their powerfulness in the world of entertainment? I had no clue why I thought that. All I knew was I liked the way he looked, sleek and well-oiled, confident and dangerous, like a futuristic boogeyman in the twenty-first century. For some reason my heart was racing as I stared at him.

"Hello, I'm the new secretary," I said, still breathing hard from running up all the steps.

There was no reaction from the tall dark-haired man. Apparently, his brain needed to be jump-started. Maybe it was just too early in the morning for anything to compute. Did I need to give him a password? Maybe he was deaf. Was he actually human?

"I'm Mr. Hope's new secretary," I said even louder, going with the deaf angle.

The dark-haired man deliberately stood there towering over me by a foot while he obviously gave me the once-over. It was a slow gaze that started at my feet up to my head. I felt a little uncomfortable, to tell you the truth. He was Mr. Big checking out Ms. Big Hair. I hoped I would pass muster.

I'm sure he was appalled by my big hair which was soldered to my head, unmoving in the breeze. Clown hair. Big curly clown hair. I wanted to melt into the concrete.

The handsome man leaned back, turned, and repeated what I had said to someone inside Mr. Hope's bedroom.

I could hear Mr. Hope say, "Oh yeah. Give her these papers so she can make a copy."

The handsome man at the door moved away and took the papers from Mr. Hope.

I was still at the top of the stairs and it was hard for me to see inside without being overtly gawking.

I did see that there was a flurry of people darting about trying to get Mr. Hope ready for his impending flight to another state. Bob's lawyer was there, going over the contract, as was his valet who was packing his clothes. I also saw the masseuse way in the back closing up his table.

Bob frequently flew around the country to do an hour or two at some resort or other venue. Each time he was paid handsomely. $100,000 a show someone had told me. Not bad for an hour or so. Also, he was flown there by Alex Spanos' pilot, for free. Someone told me it was free, but I didn't verify that factoid.

Alex was a rich man, a billionaire, and had formed a relationship with Bob which lasted through the years. They had made a deal of some sort for Alex to provide Bob with the daily use of one of Alex's planes. At the time, I didn't know who was who in Mr. Hope's room, but later came to know of each and every one of them as I worked with them.

The handsome man, who I later found out was, indeed, Mark Anthony, Bob Hope's agent. He returned to the open door and handed me the papers. This time he had a big pearly white smile on his face. I wondered who slipped him a ten-spot to be nice to me, or maybe he just got a jolt of electricity to his heart. CLEAR!

"Here you go," Mark said, still smiling as he handed me the papers.

"I'll be back," I said in my best Arnold Schwarzenegger *Terminator* voice, as I took the papers and turned and started down the steps.

Out of the blue, Bob Hope came out of his door and stepped on the balcony and yelled down to me.

"Can you find Armando? I need to talk to him."

Armando was Mr. Hope's all-around handyman who worked at the house.

I turned and replied, "I'll get him, Mr. . . . ."

BOB HOPE'S BUNGALOW: Tales From The Typing Trenches

That's when I froze, along with all time as we knew it. Butterflies froze. Birds froze. A plane overhead froze in mid-air. The whole world stopped. My mouth was open in a perfect circle, but no words came out.

I couldn't get the word "Hope" out of my mouth.

All I could do was stand there and stare up at him.

My mouth was wide open as I stood frozen staring at Mr. Hope for the very first time. Not because it was *the* Bob Hope. *Au contraire.*

It was because Bob Hope was almost naked. A naked eighty-year-old. Holy cow!

Bob stood near the door in all his glory in just a pair of white skivvies. Actually, they were teeny-weeny panties to me. Tight ones. Really tight. Too tight. My eyes bugged out of my head.

That was the last thing I needed to see at 9:30 in the morning. I was stunned, to say the least. I had never seen an eighty-year-old so unapologetically proud of his nakedness. I guess that happens in show biz. No one cares if you're dressed, undressed, half-dressed, or wearing Prada.

"Armando's probably out back," offered Mr. Hope, oblivious to my reaction to him.

The butterflies, birds, and the plane all resumed their movement.

"Oh," I whispered.

But I didn't move. I couldn't move. My eyes ran up and down his frame as he stood in the doorway.

Mr. Hope apparently picked up on my uncomfortableness and moved backwards and half-hid himself behind the door. Now I was treated to seeing half of Bob Hope, specifically his hairy leg and arm, straddling the door frame.

"Over there," said Mr. Hope, indicating with his index finger that I go to the right side of the property.

I finally snapped out of it and pulled myself together and croaked, "I'll get Armando for you."

Off I went, literally tripping down the stairs in my hurry.

As I looked back at Mr. Hope, I saw his agent, Mark Anthony, standing beside him, both grinning like a Cheshire cat at my uncomfortableness. He thought it was funny! Frighten the new girl. Mission accomplished! Who would ever believe me? Bob Hope naked? No way!

Between you and me, I couldn't get down those steps fast enough and away from the two of them. I was the proverbial fish out of water when it came to naked men and the Hollywood scene. I thought anyone over eighty years of age surely wouldn't be interested, or even be able to have sex at that age! Does a man have super powers after a certain age? Was their sex drive impervious to aging? I was of the opinion that they would slow down as they aged.

Boy, was I wrong!

Chapter 9

ARMANDO

I raced toward him on the three-hole putting green. Bob Hope was a pretty good golfer but always wanted to improve his game.

Armando was kneeling down picking up the white balls that were all around the green. His pockets were stuffed with the balls. He wiped off the dirt and tried to get them as clean as he could before putting them inside his pockets.

"Armando!" I yelled, hoping it was him. I had seen him running around but hadn't been formally introduced.

I raced toward him and the three hole putting green screaming louder, "Armando!"

"That's me!" he yelled back with a generous smile. He was short, beefy, and cute.

As I got closer, Armando tipped his cap at me and almost bowed.

It was a nice gesture. I smiled back at him.

He held out his hand to shake hands with me.

I shook it but for some reason I couldn't let go. Or maybe Armando couldn't let go. I don't know, but I was nervous. Mr. Hope said to get Armando right away and here we were shaking hands and not letting go.

"Mr. Hope wants to see you, pronto," I said. I don't know where I pulled the word 'pronto' from other than my butt. I had never used that word before.

Armando let go of my hand reluctantly.

I pointed to Mr. Hope's house, jabbing at the air.

"Quick. He will have my hide if you don't get up there right away," I stammered at him in earnest.

"Ay chihuahua. I'm going. Nice to meet you, Miss," he smiled, touching his cap again, and was off running toward Mr. Hope's bedroom.

Does everyone run when Mr. Hope says he wants to see you? Yes. He was the employer and a big star. I think Mr. Hope actually got a kick out of everyone at his beck and call, scurrying around like rats in a maze. I didn't care. It was kind of exciting in a weird sort of way. Run, run, run. Rush, rush, rush. I felt like Jerry Lewis in the film, *The Bellboy* (1960). All the rushing around was invigorating. Lord knows, I needed the exercise. The excitement was a bonus.

What can I say about Armando? He was about fifty or so, funny, charming, and had a million dollar smile. He was Mr. Hope's "handyman" and driver. He also was a big influence in my life. Armando made the job enjoyable and a lot of fun.

He was about five-foot-five, give or take, and had curly black hair, laced with a little gray at the sides.

Later, when I was at my desk, I noticed him watching me while I was on the phone. I guess he wondered what I was all about, being the new girl on the team. He stood around the file room directly in front of my desk, pretending to look for something, and kept looking out at me. He seemed friendly and had a big grin plastered on his face.

BOB HOPE'S BUNGALOW: TALES FROM THE TYPING TRENCHES

When I got off the phone, he stepped out of the file room and stood in front of my desk and said, "I forgot to welcome you to the Bungalow. In case you didn't remember, I'm Armando."

He rolled his R's with abandonment. I always liked that in a man.

"Oh yes, I remember you," I replied. "Was Mr. Hope mad for keeping him waiting?" I asked worriedly. Don't want to be fired on my first day, I thought.

"Oh no, he wasn't mad. He just wanted me to make sure we had enough of his golf balls on hand to bring to Lakeside Country Club tomorrow so he could do some golfing. He likes to golf, a lot," whispered Armando like it was a big top secret. Everyone knew Bob Hope liked to golf. He always made jokes about it in his monologues.

"You know it's about time we got a fresh face in here," he said and held out his hand to shake. "You are Miss...."

"Just call me Carol," I said and shook hands with him enthusiastically.

Again, he had my hand in an iron grasp and shook my hand continuously, his grin still in place. My body was flopping all over the place with the shaking of my hand. Armando was strong as an ox.

"If there is anything you need, call me. I'm always around." He smiled even wider.

"I'll do that," I said and laughed. I was just glad to get my hand back from him in one piece. Armando went out the back door with a wave.

In my mind, I was just hoping to get through my first day. I said to myself, Please God, don't let me need anything. I felt I had a lot to prove, especially to myself. I had to be the best secretary ever for Mr. Hope.

Armando was Hispanic with an ever-so-slight accent. He was about a couple of inches or so taller than me with curly dark hair. What impressed me the most was his big smile. His teeth were super white and really stood out. I had to have sunglasses around him. Yes, they were that bright. He was like a waiter doing everything he could to get a big tip. Yet, I liked him immediately. He had twinkling brown eyes and showed me the utmost of respect. Who does that? It was old school and I loved it.

It was nice especially when most guys give you just a grunt to acknowledge that you're in the room and think they've gone out of their way for you. Good grief, Armando treated me like a lady. I was very impressed and flattered.

Later, I learned that Armando was married and had a huge family, but Bob Hope was his life. He worked for Mr. Hope for at least thirty years. He worshipped Mr. Hope. He did everything for the man. Mr. Hope realized how special Armando was. When Armando retired, Mr. Hope threw him a party and gave him a big fat check in the thousands! In my book, that was the kindest and loveliest thing to do for an employee. It showed Mr. Hope cared.

Then again, Armando was no ordinary employee. He was like one of the family at the Hope residence.

The phone rang again. It was Bob Hope.

I took a deep breath, "Yes Mr. Hope."

"I need you to round up Armando for me again," he said.

"No problem. I'll get him for you," I said.

"I have to leave by ten," warned Mr. Hope.

Bob Hope didn't mess around with chit chat. There was no Good Morning or Hello, I'm your new boss. He just cut to the chase, Find Armando for me, asap.

While we were talking, I spotted Armando from the window.

"He's standing right outside," I said to Mr. Hope. "Do you want me to send him up to you?" I asked.

"Give me five minutes and then send him up," said Mr. Hope and immediately hung up.

As I replaced the receiver, I got up and went to the back door and waved at Armando, "Mr. Hope wants to see you in five minutes." I held up my five fingers at Armando as I stood outside with him. I breathed in the morning air and said, "I love the smell of napalm in the morning."

Armando looked over at me.

I said, "That was a line from the 1979 movie *Apocalypse Now*."

"Ah," he said. "I thought you meant the fertilizer on the grass was too strong."

"No," I laughed. "I just like quoting lines from great movies. Kind of a hobby of mine."

Armando smiled and nodded, then looked toward the Hope residence.

"I hope he'll let me drive this time," said Armando with a wry smile.

"Bob Hope does his own driving?" I asked incredulously. Bob Hope was eighty!

"Ay, chihuahua," replied Armando, making the sign of the cross across his chest.

Good Catholics all know that movement from the first moment they attended a church service. Your two fingers (or one finger) touch your head, then they touch the middle of your chest, then they touch your left arm and repeat on your right arm. Some Catholics finish with a kiss to the closed hand, or some end with a touch to the middle of your chest. I usually did the latter.

I smiled at his fearful face. I guessed that could only mean that Mr. Hope's driving scared the bejesus out of Armando.

"Do you enjoy driving him around town a lot?" I asked innocently.

"Only if I have a death wish," he grinned.

I chuckled openly. "He's that bad?" I asked.

"Bad?" Armando looked around to see if anyone was listening to our conversation.

Then he said in a lowered voice, "No one is safe on the streets when Mr. Hope gets behind the wheel. He can't see as good as he thinks he can. Sometimes we end up half on the sidewalk and half in the street as we cruise down the boulevard."

"What? But he finally pulls back onto the street, right?" I asked.

"Oh no. He's usually waving at someone and doesn't notice we're about to hit a parked car or a person waiting on the corner for the light to change. Oiy."

I loved the Yiddish mixed with the Spanish comments that came out of Armando's mouth. He was very funny. Actually, Armando became my most trusted confidante while I worked there. He made the job enjoyable and fun.

"Really? He isn't aware of oncoming traffic?" I asked, wanting to know even more.

"It's like an old Keystone Kops routine. Mr. Hope sways the car from right to left, goes through lights. The oncoming traffic dodges out of his way. I'm in the passenger seat, sweating and crying and have my rosary in my hands, praying out loud in Spanish to the Blessed Virgin Mary for help."

By now I was laughing with Armando, envisioning the slapstick scene unfolding in the car.

We snickered together as quietly as we could like conspirators for another minute.

I looked back at the Bungalow thinking I better get back to my desk.

Armando wiped his tears of laughter away and whispered to me, "I love this job and Mr. Hope, and the Blessed Virgin Mary protects us each time. It's a miracle!" He grinned at me, then looked at his watch.

"I better get over there," he said.

It was time to get Mr. Hope.

Then Armando waved at me as he walked toward Mr. Hope's stairs. It might take a few minutes to get Mr. Hope and his golf clubs down to the shiny new Chrysler parked in the driveway.

"Good luck, Armando," I said.

He turned and tossed me a grin and a thumbs-up gesture.

I went back inside toward my desk, passing Fran's office.

Frances just glared at me as I sat down at my desk. Her calculator was running the numbers nonstop. The sound of the calculator had a special rhythm all to itself. Tap, tap, pound, then a crunch sound and back to another round of tap, tap, pound.

I did not raise my eyes to look at her. I was afraid I might turn into a pillar of salt.

BOB HOPE'S BUNGALOW: Tales From The Typing Trenches

I heard the gate open, creaking like a gate in need of repair or at least a drop of 10W40. Truth be told, the gate was probably built in the 1930s.

I can hear Mr. Hope's comment now. "It still works, so why fix something that ain't broke?" Yes, Mr. Hope kept his money very close to the vest. Tightwad was a word that immediately came to mind. However, everyone had their little idiosyncrasies, and he was no different. I liked to spend. Mr. Hope liked to hoard and he was famous for it.

I never knew that Mr. Hope had a reputation for being a bad driver. I don't think anyone did except the cops in Toluca Lake. The local cops always gave Bob Hope a wide berth. It was an unwritten law that no one should give Mr. Hope a ticket for bad driving. It wouldn't look good to be arresting an 80-year-old man who entertained presidents and servicemen, who hobnobbed with industrialists and famous entertainers, and was the most well-known comedian in the world! No, the cops turned a blind eye to his bad driving willingly.

Later, I learned that Mr. Hope had serious eye problems. He had this problem in his right eye in the early 1980s. In 1982 his right eye was inflamed and hemorrhaging. Also, his left eye had similar issues and required four laser operations. His eyes were so bad he had to back out of an appearance to entertain American troops in Lebanon. Both eyes were troublesome. I never noticed the eye problems in 1983, but he may have suffered from Age-Related Macular Degeneration, which is also known as AMD.

Armando usually found a way to get Mr. Hope to relinquish the wheel and let him drive. Needless to say, Armando loved chauffeuring Mr. Hope. It was a nice diversion in the day. The two of them talked about everything from jokes to current events. Sometimes they drove over to Marie Callender's Restaurant & Bakery to pick up some delicious food or they'd go over to the local hardware store to see what was new in the world of tools. Can you imagine the King of Comedy, the Schnoz, Old Ski Nose, the Big White Hope, hammering and nailing wood together? I couldn't, either.

Sometimes Armando would just take Mr. Hope for a drive. They always ended up over at the Lakeside Golf Club in Burbank to schmooze with the wealthy golfers at the clubhouse. Wherever they went, it was always an adventure with Mr. Hope's fans hanging off his every word. Bob loved it. He was a star. Forget about winning the Oscar, he was adored by almost everyone the world over.

Armando was always by Mr. Hope's side providing companionship, friendship, and kindness. I personally thought Armando was a wonderful person. He was so sweet and caring and always had a smile. He would give you the shirt off his back. I don't think I had ever met anyone so kind. He always was in the background ready to help Mr. Hope if need be. I imagine his job was a dream job for him. He was always there, rain or shine. Everyone loved Armando. He was a real peach of a guy.

One day Armando told me a story about comedian George Burns that completely shocked me.

Apparently, George liked hot women. He didn't do anything with them. He was very old. But he sure liked to have them come over to his house in a black maid's uniform. Short, frilly black lace with plunging necklines. The kicker was that he insisted they wear no panties and turn and walk away from him with their cheeks flapping in the wind.

I said to Armando, "That's hard to believe. George Burns wants to see the butts of women but with no touching?"

Armando nodded and shrugged his shoulders. Celebrities are a breed unto themselves.

"I know it's not what you would expect to hear, but it leaves quite a picture in one's mind, doesn't it?" he said.

"Hollywood is so weird. It should have been named Holly*weird*," I said.

Armando nodded and smiled. "Just be glad you get to go home at five. Strange stuff happens at the Hope house later in the night."

I did my usual double take reaction.

"What does that mean?" I asked as Armando walked away. He wasn't about to elaborate on that topic.

"Hey, you can't just say something like that and not explain yourself. Armando, come back!" I yelled.

But he had scurried away.

I was going to get to the bottom of that scary comment, even if it killed me!

Throughout my life, my natural inquisitiveness always got me into trouble. Working for Mr. Hope proved the point.

I was born curious and was usually in the wrong place, at the wrong time, and always with the wrong person. Why would working for Bob Hope be any different?

Chapter 10

BOOK 'EM DANNO

I was invited by my girlfriends to meet them at the local Holiday Inn in Glendale for drinks on Saturday night. The Holiday Inn was a hangout of mine. It had a bar with cheap drinks and juke box music. It was an unspoken rule, that if any of us hooked up with someone special, we would find our own way home. That is what happened to me when I met Dan the cop.

Dan was so smooth and easygoing and always wore a Hawaiian shirt that I renamed him Danno to match the Hawaiian cop's name on the television series *Hawaii Five-0* (1968) which had starred Jack Lord. The name of the policeman from the old TV series, Danny, also known as Danno Williams, seemed to fit my Danno. Young, cute and fun. At the end of each TV episode you would hear actor Jack Lord say to fellow cop, played by James MacArthur, "Book 'em Danno." Even though *Hawaii Five-0* was off the air, I still referred to my cop as Danno. He would always be Big Danno to me.

BOB HOPE'S BUNGALOW: TALES FROM THE TYPING TRENCHES

I was instantly attracted to Danno's golden skin and great big happy grin. He loved everyone.

He was young, pushing thirty or so, a tall guy of Hawaiian heritage who absolutely loved to dance. His blue Hawaiian shirt was casual and festive. Nothing seemed to bother him. I liked that in a man.

"Care to dance?" he asked me holding out his hand.

How could I resist? I got up and he towered above me but that didn't stop him.

Michael Jackson's song "Beat It" was shaking the room. Tiles in the ceiling started to fall.

Danno dragged me toward the dance floor and we started to dance. It was so much fun watching this big hulk of a guy shake his booty. I did my best to keep up but clearly he was the star of the night. When the song finished, people applauded. I was laughing as he kept bowing.

"Throw money," I heard him yell out at the clapping audience. Some threw quarters, some threw straws. I even saw some cherries fly at his head. It was all in good fun.

The music changed to a slow dance and he held me close. We swayed to the music with his head resting on top of mine. He was so damn tall that my head only came up to his throat.

"Would you like a drink?" he asked. "It's on me."

"Okay," I said. "How about a Scotch and water?"

"Wow, that's hardcore," he said with a raised eyebrow.

Personally, I didn't think Scotch was *that* hardcore but I only drank it to keep from throwing up. Mixed liquor with sweet stuff in it does not agree with me. I won't tell you about the time I drank several Singapore Slings, or the time I downed three White Russians, or my favorite, Long Island Iced Tea. All of these particular drinks put me flat on my keister, drunk as a skunk, inebriated, FUBAR! To this day I can't even drink tea, thanks to the powerful Long Island Iced Tea drink that sneaks up behind you, and suddenly you're completely drunk. I'd like to punch the creator of that one. It was yummy, but deadly.

Danno and I went back to the bar area and sat down to get our drinks.

"Two Scotch and waters, please," he said to the bartender.

"So what do they call you?" I asked him.

"Just Dan. You can call me whatever you want," he said amicably.

"I like Danno," I replied, making a decision that I'd call him by that name from then on.

"Oh, so you like me?" he said as he grabbed my hand.

"What's not to like?" I flirted.

He held my hand tighter. I just smiled at him. He was absolutely charming and obviously into me.

As we bantered back and forth in this friendly conversation, I learned he was a policeman. He was definitely cute. Very tall at six-foot-four inches. Quite a contrast to me. I'm short. He was more than a foot taller than me. In actuality, he was just a little bit too tall. I'm sure we looked odd, but we didn't care.

Danno kept buying my drinks and was sort of leaning into me, an unmistakable sign of interest.

"What brings a nice girl to a den of inequity like this?" he breathed sexily.

I looked around and shrugged and said, "It's just a neighborhood bar. Nothing special."

"Maybe that's why it attracts the wrong element," he said seriously.

"You mean, you?" I laughed.

"No, take that a guy over there," he said indicating a man nursing a drink close to the door.

I looked over at the man.

"Who's he?" I asked.

"Fire Captain Orr, an Arson Investigator for Glendale Fire."

"So?"

"So, I've got a bad feeling about him. A gut feeling."

"Really? Why?" I asked curiously, while trying to get a better look at Orr.

"Just something about him. I can smell it," he said.

"Oh, so you've got a cop nose?" I teased.

"Huh?"

"You know, you have a feeling because of your cop training."

"Yeah, I guess."

"What about me? Do I have a smell?" I flirted.

"Oh, most definitely."

"I smell like a what?"

"You smell delicious," he smiled. "I could eat you up," he said and wiggled his tongue in his mouth suggestively.

"It's Chanel."

He didn't know what Chanel was, nor did he care. He just liked me. Maybe it was my dancing. Who knows?

Lionel Richie's song "All Night Long" blasted from the jukebox.

"Come on. Let's get back on the floor," he said.

He grabbed my hand and yanked me up. I didn't put up a fight. He was so cute when he danced and, besides, I loved Lionel Richie's music. It was a win-win for both of us.

We danced the night away and Danno got my number and said he was going to call me. He told me he thought I was a nice girl and his mother would be proud. I was a little tipsy and said yes to almost anything that night.

Danno followed me back to the apartment and made sure I got inside safe and sound. Nice guy, I thought. Huge and cute and way up there in the atmosphere. I didn't think we would mesh, but I liked him. I knew nothing about cops. I just had the TV shows *Hawaii 5-0* and *Starsky & Hutch* to compare them with. Sounds ridiculous, but what did I know about cops? Other than they always gave me traffic tickets. But I was open to new adventures, and new men. I was in California, the land of movie stars and where anything was possible.

The first date with Danno was a very proper date with no strings attached and no shenanigans. I guess I wanted a little more action but was afraid due to his job and his hugeness of stature. He was so polite. Danno wore another Hawaiian shirt with shorts and flip flops. It reminded me of my first date when I was fourteen years old. Sweet and innocent.

We went to Disneyland for the day and wound up making out in the boat that floated on a river in the boat ride called "It's a Small World."

We dated a few more times, then he just stopped calling. I never heard from him again. Either he went undercover on assignment or was killed. I tend to think on the bright side and hoped he was nailing a drug cartel kingpin and thus he could not contact me.

To this day, I have fond memories of Danno, but life goes on. I had my hands full of the Bob Hope craziness at the Hope house to worry about.

Chapter 11

BOB'S PEOPLE

Bob Hope had many workers which included the security guards, Armando the handyman, the masseuse, Ken from NBC, Ward the spokesman/publicist, the advertising executive with the Chrysler account, the staff writers, and, of course, Bob Hope's secretaries.

I will explain each one in more depth as you read through the book.

There were several security guards. An older guard worked the day shift on weekends, and there was another guard who worked the night shift every night. It was hard to keep track of everyone because I didn't live at the Hope house 24/7. I always talked to the guard that came on duty starting around 5:00 p.m. He was retired and was a former cop. This job was easy for him. All he had to do was protect Bob Hope and the family. The guard knew exactly what to do. He was always at the Bungalow manning the gate. As was my nature, I was friendly with everyone who worked at the Bungalow. The night shift guard and I formed an office-like friendship. He was really nice and was at least twenty-five years older than me with a great sense of humor. I think humor was the prerequisite of all the Hope workers.

When I came on board, I was young and full of piss and vinegar, as my mother would say. I was the one who was always in places I shouldn't have been, and chaos followed me everywhere. Sometimes I felt like I was starring in an *I Love Lucy* (1951) sitcom.

The male masseuse came over every day at 5:00 p.m. sharp to massage Mr. Hope. He even brought his own table with him. The masseuse got out all the kinks of the day for Mr. Hope.

Ward Grant was the publicist at Hope Enterprises and was excellent at his job. He had this great laugh which shook his whole body. He was big and bearded, and definitely one of a kind.

Ken Kantor worked at NBC and was considered another Bob Hope spokesman. I dealt with him several times. He usually was so busy he barely had time to eat lunch. I found Ken to be a genuinely nice guy.

The advertising executive was a doll. He was about ten years younger than the rest of them and very personable and friendly. He had the Chrysler account and worked with Mr. Hope who appeared in the Chrysler commercials. I remember he had a messenger bring me a huge chocolate cheesecake for Christmas. Now that's a present I can get behind! He even tried to get me a job at his agency when I resigned from the Hope job. The ad man was a really nice guy. If his agency hadn't been so far away from Glendale, I would have gone for it. Woulda coulda shoulda. One more missed opportunity.

The secretaries were on the front lines at Mr. Hope's residence in Toluca Lake. We took the calls. Calls came from the rich and famous. Calls from the music world, calls from the Military, from Presidents to Congressmen and Congresswomen. We, as workers, saw it all, and we absolutely loved it.

My job as Secretary #2 was to type the jokes, take them to Mr. Hope who made them fit his monologue and eventually I filed them. I even answered his fan mail.

BOB HOPE'S BUNGALOW: Tales From The Typing Trenches

It wasn't a glamorous job. We just showed up and answered the phones and typed letters. Most of all we typed up the jokes from the staff writers.

The writers were the kings and queens. The time I worked there at Mr. Hope's house, I met Bob's first female on-staff writer, Martha Bolton. She paved the way for other female writers.

But there was another female writer that I found most amusing. Kathy Green adored Bob Hope. She gave away her jokes to him and I know he used some of them on his TV specials. Maybe he paid her but I never asked.

Kathy Green wasn't on staff when I worked at the Bungalow, but I think she should have been. I do know that Kathy was a really funny lady. She told me stories about her and her sister that had me in tears of laughter.

I remember going to lunch with her one day. Kathy had this old car which had really bad springs. When I say bad, I mean the worst in the world. Every time Kathy drove over a pothole in the ground, the car bounced up in the air like a Mexican low rider and bounced and bounced down the street. The car springs were so bad I flew up in the air and my head hit the car roof top. It almost knocked me out. Yes, it hurt like hell. I tried to laugh it off but I have an indentation in my skull the size of Pittsburgh which is still there almost four decades later. You can't cover it up. It still looks like a landing field in need of repair.

The band of brothers and sisters of the jokes were an amazing bunch. I don't know how they came up with a barebones topic and just made light of it. These writers were incomparable.

There is an art to joke telling starting with the mundane, building the middle and then POW! You end with a surprise, an unexpected punch at the end. It is an art form that you try to figure out where it's going to end, but the fun is the surprise or the climax of the joke. Funny stuff. Stuff teachers try to teach, but unless you've got that mind that can twist it just right and catch the listener off guard, it is hard to learn. There is a simplicity and a beauty to a joke. We all join in waiting for the punchline, anticipating, begging it to happen, and when it does, it's rhapsody. It's relief. It's almost as good as sex! I say that because I love jokes so much. I love to laugh so hard that I can't breathe. My brain is in a fog with the punchline within reach. It's almost too much to put into words. I laugh until my stomach aches. I have tears streaming down my face. My mouth hurts from smiling. I am spent! That's the power of a great joke.

These jokesters, these gag writers, these lovers of words turned on their side, are the lifelines of comedians everywhere.

Writing a joke is not easy. Writing a topical one is harder. Writing on a deadline for a huge star is monumental!

All I can say, dear writers, is thank you for making me cry with laughter at your humor.

Chapter 12

KATHY

Kathy was the Head Secretary, also known as Secretary # 1. She was taller than me, but then who wasn't? She was a lot older. She had been a celebrity assistant for years. Her hair was still dark with salt and pepper wisps of gray throughout. Although she had a trim figure, I could see that life had beaten her down. She had a slight slump to her shoulders but an easy smile. She had been hired before me and usually took dictation from Mr. Hope way into the night. She had worked for celebrities before but didn't dress the part. I assumed she didn't buy flashy clothes so that her celebrity bosses could shine. She and Mr. Hope were "tight" and she and he worked late. My job was 9 to 5 and her job started at 10 until 7 or later. I actually was glad that I was Secretary # 2 because I hated to work into the wee hours of the night. I was an early riser and wanted to go home at five o'clock. When you work for a celebrity that does not happen. After all, they are the boss and when you're needed to work late, you do. I always thanked God that I got to go home at five. Sometimes being #2 has its perks.

I thought Kathy and I did essentially the same job. Type the jokes, answer the phones and help Mr. Hope get ready for his daily "smokers" that he attended every night in any state that signed him up to be the comedian on the bill. A smoker is a venue that mostly gentlemen attended, whether it be in a club or a private venue. The jokes for these smokers were much more raunchier than his television shows that were typically aimed at families. The writers tailored the off-color jokes toward men who essentially liked dirty jokes. There was nothing wrong with that. The off-color jokes were just aimed at a more rough and tumble crowd. They were actually funnier than the jokes Bob told on air. Mr. Hope made an average of $100,000 per gig when I worked there. He would fly out every night to another venue with fresh jokes from his stable of writers. Essentially, those writers were on call 24/7. If Bob had an idea, whether it was in the day or the middle of the night, he'd call Gene or Robert and ask them to come up with more jokes on the topic. Bob Hope wanted to see the jokes first thing in the morning so there was no sleeping in. I'll tell you more about the writers later. They were a trip!

Kathy was very cordial and kind. She never lost her cool.

She didn't dress flashy. She just wore the usual dress and a sweater. She had a deep voice which was sultry and inviting. Some of the writers thought they were talking to her when, in fact, they were speaking with me. I guess I had the same voice as her. I could tell the difference between us but others could not. The tone we had was a calming tone with a dash of sexiness to sweeten the deal. I don't know if I copied Kathy because I didn't change my style of speaking. I think we were low talkers like a character on Jerry Seinfeld's television show. Whatever the reason, we talked the same, and people related to it. I think we were friendly and helpful in a kind way to those on the phones. Robert told me he could tell us apart in that I had a higher lilt to my voice once I started speaking. I'm not sure what that meant, but I went with it. Sometimes I would try to speak lower than usual just to mix things up.

BOB HOPE'S BUNGALOW: Tales From The Typing Trenches

Towards the end of my year's tour of duty, Kathy wanted a few days off from work and told Mr. Hope he could use me over the weekend. I waited all Saturday for his call, but it never came. I usually walked down to my favorite restaurant in Glendale, the Salt Shaker, and had a bite to eat. At 2:30 p.m. I was hungry and hadn't heard from Mr. Hope, so I went for a late lunch.

The Salt Shaker was packed, as usual, and I took my time. I ran into an old friend and we got to talking over coffee and before you knew it, it was after four o'clock. When I got back to my apartment, there was a message on my answer machine from the security guard at the Hope residence. My heart sank. I knew I had to go to work late Saturday night. I was depressed and returned the security guard's number. As I listened to the older guard, I heard him say that Mr. Hope had decided to go golfing instead. Wow, I was off the hook! I didn't hear anything on Sunday either. I lucked out, I thought.

When Kathy came in Monday at 10:00 a.m., she told me the security guard had called her at home when he didn't get ahold of me. She told him she was unavailable to come in due to prior plans. That's when Mr. Hope gave up and went golfing at Lakeside Golf Club.

Essentially, that was the end of it, or so I thought.

Chapter 13

MARIE, NIXON, AND FORD

Marie was the assistant to Nancy, the office manager. She had bouffant blonde hair and was about five-foot-ten inches tall. Talk about a sense of humor. She would say things that made me do a double take. The off-the-cuff remarks that came out of her mouth were hilarious. At first I asked myself, did I hear her right? She was deadpan funny. I had to watch her for a moment and then I saw the little smile start to curl up on her lips. She knew she was funny and was checking to make sure people got her joke. From then on, I was always waiting for one of her comments when everything and everyone around us was going mad and she never failed me. I guess that's what happens when you work around the Bob Hope people. They say and do things that literally crack you up. Marie knew everything that was going on at the house. She had her ear to the ground like Radar from the TV show *M*A*S*H* (1972) and absorbed everything. She wasn't loud or boisterous. There was a quiet calm to her, tinged with a devilish sense of humor. I learned an awful lot from Marie's demeanor and was the better for it. You can be a nice person in Hollywood and live to tell about it!

Marie sat up front, closest to the Dutch door where everyone entered the Bungalow. She guarded that door like an army sergeant. No one got inside until they had passed inspection by Marie. She was still sweet and nice, but you had to have a reason to get beyond the double Dutch door.

For the uninitiated, with a Dutch door you are able to open the top half of the door and see who is outside. The bottom half of the door remained locked for security reasons until it was safe to let in the visitors. It was popular years ago but I think it might be coming back in vogue.

As I said before, my initial reaction to Marie was that she was a hoot!

One of the first things I remember about her was her favorite anecdote that she told me about the door.

One day she heard a soft knocking on the double Dutch door and got up to answer it. This was one of her jobs, to make sure no one barged into the Bungalow. She only opened the top part of the Dutch door and looked out.

No one was there. Marie looked down the driveway. No one was seen. She shook her head and started to close the top part of the door.

"It's me," said the tiny voice.

Marie opened the top door again. She frowned. No one was there.

"Down here," piped up the little voice.

Marie looked down.

It was Billy Barty on tippy toes looking up at her. He was a Little Person and very funny. He worked a lot in the business and knew everyone.

"I didn't see you there," Marie said, staring at him with a smile on her face.

"No one ever does," he replied. He was joking, of course.

"Are you here for Mr. Hope?" she asked.

He nodded.

She let him in and called Mr. Hope on the phone. He told her to let Billy in. Marie walked Billy through the Bungalow and along the driveway and toward Mr. Hope's bedroom in the main house.

Later, she would retell that tale to anyone who wanted to hear it. It was a funny story.

I had heard it several times and still laugh at it now. Each time Marie embellished the story with her acting skills. Everything got grander and wilder with each retelling. I never got tired of her "stories."

Marie was also fond of retelling the Nixon landing in Mr. Hope's backyard. I had heard of it but Marie described it in minute detail complete with sound effects similar to the Vietnam war-time helicopter landing in *The Killing Fields* (1984).

Apparently, the then-President Richard Nixon wanted to see Bob Hope. He wasn't your usual president at the White House in the 1980s, in that momentous things happened to Richard Nixon, like the Watergate Scandal. Remember that?

Anyway, Nixon had prepared to meet with Mr. Hope, but he didn't want to just drive over. No way! He had his pilot drop him off from an Army helicopter into Mr. Hope's Toluca Lake backyard. Can you hear the rumblings of the helicopter blades? It forced all the neighbors outside, thinking they were being invaded.

Marie said the noise from the chopper's blades was deafening. Everyone stared out the windows at the landing, watching Nixon emerge and duck down to avoid being sliced by the chopper's blades. Then he and his entourage ran, bent over, toward the Hope house. I wasn't there to see this, but with Marie's detailed description of events that day, I felt I was there. Apparently, Nixon's landing made all the papers as well as the local TV news media in Burbank.

Former President Nixon was always big news. He certainly knew how to make an entrance!

I would be remiss if I didn't mention former President Gerald Ford. I found Jerry Ford to be a real gentleman.

Mr. Hope was on another call, but former President Ford wanted to hold on the line with me. I learned that since leaving the White House, Jerry Ford was very proud of building the Gerald R. Ford Presidential Library and Museum. The Library was located in Ann Arbor, Michigan on the north campus of the University of Michigan. The Museum portion was about 130 miles away in Grand Rapids, Michigan. While talking to him on the phone, I thought Jerry Ford was just like one of the boys, down to earth, friendly, and chatty. He definitely loved golf, whether he beaned anybody with a golf ball or not was another story. Fore!

"How much longer do you think Bob's going to be?" Jerry asked me.

"When he's talking to stars like Brooke Shields or Ann Jillian, it could be awhile. But, since he's on with Richard Nixon, I'm sure he'll be off in a minute," I replied.

"So he'd rather talk to pretty girls than Nixon?" asked Jerry. He was amused.

"Wouldn't you?" I said, like President Ford was an everyday Joe Blow on the other end of the line.

"I plead the fifth on that one," said Jerry. "Don't want to get in trouble with Betty," he laughed.

I could tell that Mr. Hope was not on the phone with Nixon any longer.

"Mr. Hope is finally off the phone," I said to Jerry. "Let me transfer you now."

"Remember, don't mention what I said about pretty girls to Betty," he whispered to me.

"You got it, Mr. President. Mum's the word," I whispered back to him and then quickly transferred Jerry to Mr. Hope.

Thinking back, even Presidents get a little nervous when it comes to their wives, and aren't they the real power in Washington?

The following is an old joke Mr. Hope loved to tell about President Ford.

"I bumped into Gerald Ford the other day and said pardon me."

To which, Ford muttered, "I don't do *that* anymore."

For those who don't remember, President Ford pardoned Richard Nixon for his part in the Watergate scandal, which didn't sit too well with the public or Congress at the time. Just saying.

Chapter 14

NANCY

The Office Manager, Nancy, was an attractive tall blonde who dressed appropriately for the office. She was always in a dress and worked as Mrs. Hope's personal secretary as well. She was a professional with a quiet voice. I liked her when I first met her. She had an easy smile and made a lot of the administrative decisions.

She also had a sensitive nature. Marie told me that Mrs. Hope could get grouchy and took out her frustrations on poor Nancy. I got the feeling that Marie hated the way Mrs. Hope treated Nancy.

Nancy and Marie also helped out with autographs that the fans wanted. Mr. Hope was a very busy man and a lot of the time the office staff did his autographing.

I had my hands full with all the phone calls from celebrities, business people who wanted to speak to Bob, and I had to screen the calls. Everyone had their job at the Bungalow. We were busy all day, every day.

BOB HOPE'S BUNGALOW: Tales From The Typing Trenches

Nancy also had an older volunteer named Barbara who loved helping out when it came to envelope stuffing and other office work, like opening the fan mail. She was so nice and always smiling. All three of them at the front got along famously. Kathy and I were the secretaries in the back room who directly answered to Mr. Hope and worked with the writers, typing the jokes as fast as our little fingers would allow, and then delivering them upstairs to him. This was serious work at the Hope house. Jokes took precedence over everything. You might say they were Mr. Hope's bread and butter.

In general, it was a very busy office every single day. The constant typing, the phones ringing off the hook, the visitors, and the non-stop commotion, was exhilarating to me.

I remember Christmas as being wild with all the Christmas cards that Mr. Hope sent out to his celebrity friends, family, agents, writers, and other entertainment giants of the day. He hired a company to stuff these Christmas cards into hand-addressed envelopes which ran in the thousands. Talk about blowing a fortune at the post office. However, that was considered part of the job.

The other part was the filing of the jokes. There were so many files and folders in the two vaults. Jokes were by topic and writer and had to be in both files. Many a time Mr. Hope called wanting me to find a joke on a certain topic. Usually, I found it without a problem. The filing system was rudimentary, but we knew exactly where to find the joke he wanted to review. There was no computer system, just hand-typed Xeroxed copies of jokes everywhere in the files.

Some of Bob Hope's earliest jokes were found duplicated on that black carbon paper which is *really* "old school."

I'd estimate there were close to a million jokes, maybe more. Jokes were Bob's living and he treated each one of them like precious jewels. I have to agree with him. These jokes were precious, priceless, and above all, knee-slapping funny. They now are historically preserved in the Library of Congress.

Chapter 15

MILTON

So many callers tried to speak to Bob Hope. If he knew the person, it was just a matter of putting the call through. Because we answered with just a "Hello," it was hard to know who they had reached. Reporters calling or visiting the Hope house were almost non-existent during my time. After all, Bob was eighty and on the down side of the mountain. However, Bob still had a lot of phone calls that Kathy and I screened. Celebrities to world leaders to retired politicians to writers and wrong numbers would call in daily. I had to find out who they were before I put them through to Mr. Hope. Usually, I recognized everyone by name, but there was one who stumped me completely.

The phone rang and I just answered "Hello" in my deepest voice.

The caller said, "It's Milton."

I drew a blank.

Milton? Milton who, I wondered to myself.

BOB HOPE'S BUNGALOW: TALES FROM THE TYPING TRENCHES

"Milton," I said slowly out loud. "Milton," I repeated his name again to myself. The wheels were churning inside my brain, but nothing was coming out. Milton, the doctor? The chiropractor? The reporter? The writer? A relative? A golfing buddy? I was stumped.

"Milton, you know, like in Uncle Miltie," explained the frustrated caller.

A beat, then it dawned on me. In fact, it was like a bomb explosion going off in my head. It was Milton Berle! I actually shouted his name out loud like I was on a game show, jumping out of my chair.

Milton Berle was one of the old-time comedians who had a television show for years on the network. His career also spanned over eighty years. He started out in silent films, a child actor on stage, then radio, and movies, like the hilarious movie, *It's a Mad, Mad, Mad, Mad World* (1963), and other TV appearances. He had his own television show, "The Milton Berle Show," from 1948 to 1956, and was on "Dean Martin's Celebrity Roast" from 1974 to 1984. There were endless TV shows and movies that he was in. Google him. He was a very funny man until the end in 2002.

Getting back to my story, it finally dawned on me who Milton was.

"Ohhhh, Uncle Miltie! Milton Berle! Of course!" I yelled into the phone, laying it on real thick.

I don't know why I was yelling, except I was a little excited at the time. I wanted him to know I remembered he was still a big star. Truth be told, I had never seen his show where he referred to himself as Uncle Miltie.

"That's right," said Milton, fully satisfied that I knew who he was.

"Let me transfer you right away, Mr. Berle!" I shouted again.

People who were near me started to wonder why I was yelling.

I quickly put Milton Berle on hold and feverishly dialed Mr. Hope and announced, "It's Milton Berle!"

"Oh yeah, Milton," said Mr. Hope like he was an every day caller. He was NOT!

"Put him through," said Bob impatiently.

I immediately transferred Milton to Mr. Hope by jiggling the receiver.

I didn't hear anything so I said, "Hello?"

"Still waiting," said Milton sarcastically.

I had not transferred Milton over to Mr. Hope's line. All that jiggling must have canceled out everything. I was so nervous that Milton would curse me out, or worse, hang up. I was sweating bullets.

I kept praying to myself as I toggled the phone's receiver again. Please God, don't let me screw this up.

I couldn't disconnect Uncle Miltie! I was shaking as I waited for the two of them to talk to each other. Then finally, it worked! They were connected!

"Milton!" shouted Bob into the phone.

"Bob!" shouted Milton.

I breathed a sigh of relief. They were now connected and speaking to each other like old buddies meeting after the war.

"Man, it's like trying to break into Fort Knox to reach you!" shouted Milton. "I thought your secretary was going to ask me for the secret password!"

"We don't just let anyone through," laughed Bob.

I quickly disconnected myself by hanging up. No sense in listening in to comments about my secretarial skills.

After the transfer, I put my head on the desk, breathing heavily. I finally did it! I was a little embarrassed that I didn't recognize Milton Berle's voice. What was wrong with me? I knew all the TV and movie stars' voices. I was a professional celebrity secretary, after all.

Kathy was watching me with a half smile. I'm sure she had an inkling of what had transpired, but never said a word.

In my mind, I had pulled it off and no one at the Bungalow knew I didn't know Uncle Miltie was Milton Berle. Thank God I dodged that bullet! I must have sweated off five pounds of worry that day.

Chapter 16

AT THE PLAYBOY CLUB

My weekends were mine. I didn't think about work or jokes or Bob Hope.

One Saturday night, I was asked out by Rick, a former office associate who had worked for the same law firm as my old boss. He said he knew everybody who was anybody in Hollywood. I doubted that. Rick was always trying to impress me but rarely did. I asked him if he knew anyone at the Playboy Club since I had heard a lot about the place.

Now let me explain before everybody goes off half-cocked. I didn't want to see any bunnies, nor did I want to try out to be in a *Playmate* spread. I was just curious and since I was in Los Angeles, why not see what the Playboy Club was all about? You should try anything once, right?

I knew Rick wanted to impress me. He said he had two tickets to the Playboy Club on Saturday night. I was game and we were all dressed up in our finest. Rick, whose father owned a car dealership, drove up to my place in a baby blue 1976 convertible two-seater Mercedes-Benz 450SL. I was impressed even if it was eight years old. The car was sweet.

We drove along Sunset Strip, the breeze blowing through our hair, ready for a night on the town. I'm sure Rick thought this would secure a place in my bed with him, but he was in for a sad surprise.

Rick had borrowed the Playboy member card from his friend to get into the Club. It seemed like a good idea at the time. What could happen?

The Club was packed. While we were seated and waiting for our drinks, we watched the black comic who was the entertainment of the night, do his bit. He laid it on thick and many of the jokes were a little bit off-color, no pun intended. But the comic was definitely funny, and I laughed a lot. Probably too much, and too loud. I couldn't help it. I liked to laugh.

Rick and I sat right up front directly under the watchful eyes of the comic. So what does the comic do, but point out that I was the youngest woman in the club. Even if that was true, I didn't want to be singled out. The comic went on and on about my naivety and youth, that I was starting to turn red. I HATE being made fun of because I try my hardest to keep a low profile and not stand out.

Right about then, the waitress came over and said she wanted to see Rick's I.D. The name didn't match Rick's credit card. Rick was embarrassed and asked to speak to the waitress in private so he could explain to her that he was just trying to impress me and could she let it go just this once. Of course I had heard the entire conversation because they were only a few feet away. Why do people assume that I can't hear? Needless to say, I was slightly embarrassed at the scene Rick was causing by pleading with the waitress. Fortunately, she did let it slide but Rick had to pay cash if he wanted to stay.

Rick sheepishly came back to the table and whispered to me that he had to make a phone call and then he left the table again. The comic noticed that I was all alone and honed in on me with questions like: "Why did my boyfriend leave? Are you left paying for the bill? Why would anyone leave a young thing like you alone?" I felt like there was a huge spotlight pointed directly at me. I just smiled and saw Rick at the back and waved to him. The comic also started to wave at Rick. Everyone did.

Into his microphone the comic yelled, "Hey man! Yeah, you on the phone! Your date is waiting all alone at the table. Either you get back here or she is going home with me!"

I turned all shades of red. Then Rick came back to the table and sat down, like no big deal. The comic was not going to let things slide. He kept on teasing Rick for ignoring me and why wasn't he being more attentive. I was ready to scream. I can't tell you how much I hate being the center of attention, especially at the Playboy Club! I wanted to get out of there so bad it hurt.

Rick drove me home with the lame ass explanation as to why he used his friend's club membership and kept apologizing to me. There were no words I could find. I was done. Maybe the teasing was just too much, but the lying by Rick was worse. Needless to say, Rick and I never went out again. He was embarrassed. I was embarrassed. It just was a bad scene all around.

So much for bunnies. They are only good at Easter and only if they are the chocolate ones from Switzerland.

The comic's comments at the Playboy Club still stung, but I knew it was all in good fun, I guess. What I do know for certain is that I was never going back to the Playboy Club. Lesson learned. I just didn't belong, which is the story of my life.

Chapter 17

THE MILITARY

Mr. Hope loved to play to the Military, those G.I.'s that fought for us in World War II, and in Vietnam. They, above all, needed to laugh. They were Bob's audience. He loved them and they loved him back. There is so much footage of the military men and women piled around a make-shift stage somewhere in a dangerous part of the world, where they are laughing at Bob Hope telling jokes and bringing out the most beautiful women in the world to help him entertain the troops.

On a personal level, I had never seen anything like it. I was so moved by these wonderful guys who wrote to Bob Hope thanking him for showing up for them on foreign bases all over the world.

Then there was the military man who made a three-hour trip up from San Diego to Toluca Lake to ask for something he could use at a celebrity auction on the base. I know Mr. Hope loved these military guys and gals, as he called them, and wanted to make them laugh in the worst way, which he did. The writers were always asked to write jokes specifically tailored to the Military.

One of the writers told me Bob Hope wanted to go to these deadly foreign places and cheer on the troops and if he was caught in the crossfire, so be it. Going out in a blaze of glory while entertaining the troops would be Mr. Hope's ultimate ticket to immortality.

When I got to type up the jokes, I felt I was also doing my part for the Military, albeit a very tiny portion of it. But it felt good and I liked to help in any way I could. Our G.I.'s are the greatest and best in the world, and we all thank them for their service to their country.

Chapter 18

THE HOUSE WAS HAUNTED

The night I found out that Bob Hope's kitchen inside his house was haunted was the night I started to believe in spirits. Actually, I believed the whole Hope house was haunted!

Sure, it was common knowledge that strange things went on at Mr. Hope's house, especially in the back of the house where the kitchen was. The public didn't know, but the staff was keenly aware of it.

Armando said he heard voices in the kitchen one evening and when he went in to see who it was, there was no one there. It gave him the creeps.

Marie had told me some of the secretaries before me had heard strange sounds also.

Unearthly sounds.

None of this was plausible to me until one fateful night.

I had stayed late again to catch up on some filing and to straighten up my area. It was a mess. Kathy was off that night so she wasn't around.

BOB HOPE'S BUNGALOW: TALES FROM THE TYPING TRENCHES

Armando was still up at the house doing some work for Mr. Hope. Everyone had gone home in the Bungalow except for the security guard. He was bored, doing a crossword puzzle when I stepped outside into the compound where the Hope house was to get some air.

The back of the Bungalow overlooked the darkened lawn area where Nixon had landed his helicopter several months ago. It wasn't too far from the Par-3 putting green that Mr. Hope had put in for him to practice his putting. I liked the look and smell of freshly-clipped grass.

I was taking in the calm night air which was unseasonably warm at that time of year. If I were a smoker, I would have been lighting up. There weren't any sounds except those that came from the kitchen up at the Hope house. Clanging of pots and pans, plates put on the table, and the like. The elderly cook was humming away. I enjoyed her sounds as I stood outside. It felt homey.

The Hope's cook was busy preparing for an eight o'clock meal for the Hope family, which consisted of only Mr. and Mrs. Hope. All the children were grown adults with lives of their own. The Hopes still had their meals in the dining room, like your everyday family. Only this was a famous and rich family who had the best of the best. Cooks, maids, butlers, fine China dishes, and other trappings of the wealthy. I would say it was the Upstairs part of the home. The staff was the Downstairs part of it.

Like Armando, the cook was Hispanic. She was in the process of taking food from the kitchen into the dining room to place on the dining room table for the evening meal. It sure smelled good as the aroma of cooking wafted my way. I walked over toward the kitchen door and peeked in.

I could see a sideboard with dishes of meat and potatoes, as well as some vegetables on another huge plate.

Beyond that was a separate table covered with cooling chocolate chip cookies all lined up row upon row. I guess the cook had prepared these cookies for some dinner or event that Mrs. Hope was going to go to this coming week. I wasn't sure because those events were under the auspices of Nancy.

I opened the door to the kitchen intending to just snag one of the cookies. I was starving and the cookies were just too tempting. I confess, I'm a chocoholic to the bone. Hovering over the cookies, I was about to lift one of them from the cooling tray.

As I was hovering, the lights in the kitchen flickered. In fact, they dimmed. I looked around but saw nothing unusual.

Then I almost jumped out of my skin! I thought I had seen a face in the glass from the cupboards. I walked over and warily looked at the glass. There wasn't anything there. I spun around quickly. All quiet on the western front. I told myself to get a grip. There aren't any ghosts. Concentrate on the cookies. Forget about ghosts. They do not exist, or so I told myself.

Suddenly a breeze blew into the kitchen, causing the blinds to rattle and move, giving me pause. Can ghosts fly in on breezes, I wondered? My eyes were bugging out of my head. My heart was pounding.

As I was worrying about ghosts, Armando snuck up behind me, tapped my shoulder and said, "Boo!" all at the same time.

I sucked in a mouthful of air and spun around in fear. My eyes were big as saucers as I assumed a killer Karate stance, with my hands poised to strike. Then I saw Armando's mischievous face grinning from ear to ear.

"Armando! You scared the crap out of me!" I scolded him in a whisper, holding my hand over my heart.

It didn't matter. He thought it was funny and laughed even harder.

"Do you want a couple of them?" he asked me, indicating the cookies.

By now I had calmed myself.

"Only one. I've got to maintain my girlish figure," I said grinning back at him. I was really skinny in those days.

Armando beckoned me toward the table. He started to pick up a couple of cookies and held them out to me as he leaned on the table. What could I do? I had to be polite and take them.

As I moved toward the table to reach for the cookies, I must have inadvertently kicked the leg of the table and it started to give way. I froze.

BOB HOPE'S BUNGALOW: TALES FROM THE TYPING TRENCHES

I will never forget the look on Armando's face of pure fear. He stared at me. I stared at him. The creaking got louder. Then I heard the sound of a snap. My eyes bugged out of my head. I felt like Lucy when anything and everything goes so wrong!

"Oh no!" I uttered and dove toward the table holding it up with my hands on each side. The leg of the table was dangling and of no use at all.

The chocolate chip cookies were now moving in a "V" toward me. I was holding the table and couldn't stop them even though I tried to block them with my face. They kept coming.

Armando also tried to block the cookies from moving but they had a mind of their own and kept sliding toward me.

Armando started to push the fastest ones into his mouth. I also tried this ploy. Soon my mouth was as full as Armando's. We were like those squirrels outside in the trees that jammed nuts into their mouths causing their cheeks to bulge outward.

A row of cookies had pressed up against my stomach. I started to grab them and stuff them into my pockets to prevent them from falling off the table and onto the kitchen floor. Soon both of my pockets were overflowing with cookies.

Armando's pockets were full as well.

Then we both heard the cook walking back toward the kitchen.

Our eyes locked in fear. She couldn't catch us in this position!

Armando gestured rapidly at me with his hand to get out of there.

"Run!" he whispered.

He didn't want me to incur the wrath of the cook or be caught in the kitchen. I was supposed to have been gone at five!

I let go of the table as Armando moved into position to hold the table, and I started to back away into the dark passageway leading to the door. As I reached the passageway, I stopped, frozen in place.

From my vantage point I saw the two big guard dogs standing in my way with wicked looks on their faces. I was trapped! In my mind I was hearing those catchy song lyrics play over and over. *Who let the dogs out? Who? Who? Who?*

The two dogs were standing in front of me, looking at me, quietly growling, with their hackles up, letting tiny droplets of foam splatter onto the ground. I knew enough about dogs to know that meant they were ready to attack. Without breathing, I backed up and turned to the left and jammed my body as far as I could into the wall. It was dark in that little space and my heart was beating a mile a minute. This is the end, I thought, steeling myself for the inevitable.

The cook was now in the kitchen and saw Armando holding up the broken table leg and that he was covered in chocolate chip cookies. She let out a small squeak of dismay and then angrily started to rattle off a tirade of Spanish remarks at Armando as her hand hit the table. It wasn't so loud that the Hopes could hear, but her tone was unmistakably angry.

I can only guess that the cook was cursing him out for ruining her cookies. Half of the cookies were on the floor, the other half were in Armando's pockets and/or smeared over his face. He spoke back to her in rapid-fire Spanish. Rat a tat tat! It was impossible trying to figure out what they were saying, but I think Armando was going to get his butt kicked by her since he was the only culprit in plain sight.

Me? I was holding my breath as the dogs started to sniff and get closer to me. Nothing like having a good wet dog nose. These dogs could smell the chocolate aroma oozing from my pockets and wanted a treat in the worst way. As all good dog lovers know, you can't just give a dog chocolate, cookie or not. The dog could die from it. Chocolate is not good. Hey, I could die from the chocolate, too, especially when two dogs are on the hunt for food and growling to boot!

As I was thinking of all these issues, the white dog, Snowjob, stood up on his hind legs and held that pose in front of me. His teeth were barred which was troubling as I watched him put his two white paws on my hip. I dare not move a muscle, I thought, standing like a statue.

Now the other black dog, Shadow, decided he, too, wanted to do this little dance with me and stood up on his haunches. It was funny to see two dogs on their haunches poised in front of me. It was like they were somehow pointing directly at me. I was the guilty one in the house. Look over here everybody! We caught her!

I managed to pull out one of the cookies from my pocket, and flung it toward the door. Both dogs raced after the cookie and slid across the floor with their claws trying to stop in front of the cookie. They both tried to snap at the cookie and started growling at each other and fighting over it.

As I was holding up the wall, I heard the cook gathering up the serving dishes and still grumbling at Armando. She headed back to the dining room with the two dinners for Mr. and Mrs. Hope.

Armando immediately turned around and grabbed me and we both raced outside with the two dogs following us in hot pursuit. We must have smelled like giant Snickers bars to them since we both were carrying chocolate chip cookies in our pockets.

"I'm going to distract the security guard while you slip out the door to your car," whispered an animated Armando in my ear.

I nodded in silence. Guilty is, as guilty does. And I was SO guilty.

Armando pushed me into the Bungalow where I went flying across the floor in free fall.

He cringed but didn't have time to worry about me and moved back outside and over to the gate.

I heard Armando whistling to the guard to get his attention and asked the guard to open the gate.

While the guard and Armando were talking, I grabbed my purse from my desk and then tiptoed outside and silently moved toward my parked car at the end near the street. I ducked down quickly because the outdoor lights in the parking area started to come on like lights from a prison. The lights scanned the property looking for escapees like me. This was like a scene out of *The Great Escape* (1963). How was I going to avoid the lights as they moved toward me? There was nowhere to hide from the lights. All I could do was duck down into the plants that lined the driveway.

Armando kept talking to the guard who glanced my way. But there was nothing to see because I was kneeling down hiding from his line of sight.

As the guard turned back to Armando, I crept into my car, ducked down, and pulled on the brake handle. My Firebird started to move backwards because it was parked on the incline of the driveway. It slid slowly down the small incline onto Moorpark Street. Thankfully, no one was around. I hadn't turned on the car lights yet for fear that the security guard would see them. As my car silently rolled to a stop, I sat up and looked around. There were no cars, no pedestrians, and no street lights. I was literally out of sight. I pulled on my headlights, started my car, and drove quickly to the corner. Thank you, Armando, for your quick thinking. My pockets were still full of chocolate chip cookies which I enjoyed on my way home to Glendale. However, I regretted eating them so fast because I had terrible indigestion that night!

When I finally got into bed, after chugging a bottle of Pepto Bismol, I fell asleep instantly and dreamed I was walking through the darkened Hope kitchen looking for something and headless spirits of vaporized beings zoomed by me, flying up and down, like the Roadrunner cartoon character. They dive-bombed me, hurling chocolate chip cookies at me, shooting flames from their nostrils. At the end, I was hit by a grenade which exploded into a million little pieces of fiery chocolate shrapnel that eventually burned themselves out as they lay on the tiled kitchen floor. I had these nightmares for months, especially around the fourth of July.

I had lots of other nightmares besides the crazy headless spirit dreams.

The snarling, toothy dogs would be nipping at my heels as I ran down the driveway. Barking and nipping and snarling, those dogs were always on my mind. I always woke up with a start, and sat up in bed with sweat oozing out of every pore. I looked at the back of my pajamas to check for holes from the dogs chomping on my butt. I never found any, except in my dreams.

I really didn't get a good night's sleep until after I had left the Bob Hope job. No more dreaming of my fear of dogs who were out to chomp into my delicate skin and thirstily drink my thick red blood. No more crunching on my bones. No more dogs!

At least, no more *biting* dogs!

Chapter 19

THE JOKE MEISTERS

There was a story that made the rounds for years about a writer who was employed by Mr. Hope. He went to Hawaii on his honeymoon with his new bride fully intending to relax and get some rest and relaxation, also known as R & R.

Bob called him at his hotel room and said he needed twenty jokes as soon as possible. Needless to say the writer's nose got bent out of joint. He was on his honeymoon for God's sake! When he originally agreed to work for the Big Schnoz, also known as Bob Hope, he thought he would get a few days off for good behavior. But as he found out, there was no way he could escape Mr. Hope. When you sign on to be a gag writer for Mr. Hope, you are at Bob Hope's beck and call, twenty-four hours a day, seven days a week, into infinity. Vacation wasn't in the dictionary. R & R was only for soldiers. Comedy writers were his employees and if they wanted to keep their jobs, they were "on call" ready to write whenever the mood struck Mr. Hope. In addition, they better have the best jokes ready or else. There always was another comedy writer hungry to work for Mr. Hope. He was their lord and master. Dedication to Hope was key.

The newly-married writer managed to write twenty jokes and send them off via fax to Mr. Hope and still have time to be with his new wife. Surely he could wait to give her his undivided attention for 15 minutes or so. It would take that long for Mr. Hope to go over the material and get back to him. If the writer played his cards right, the jokes didn't need polishing or reworking, so he had better get it right the first time. Giving up a tiny bit of your honeymoon wouldn't be that difficult, would it? All you have to do is dedicate your life to Bob come rain or shine. So what if you got married? There were always plenty of girls around, but only one Bob Hope!

The other infamous joke was about when Mr. Hope called a writer at home late one night and got the writer's wife on the phone. Hope asked for the writer to come to the phone. The wife shrieked and said that her husband had told her he had to drive over to Bob Hope's and spend the night working with him on jokes. Why then was Bob Hope calling for him? Mr. Hope covered beautifully and said, "Oh yeah, that's right. Here he comes. I forgot he was taking a break. God, my memory is going. Sorry to disturb you." Mr. Hope quickly hung up on the wife, thinking he had covered for the husband, who he assumed was out cheating on his wife. Turns out that the wife had cooked up the whole scenario, tricking Mr. Hope into lying because her husband was sitting in bed with her all along! It's a funny commentary on how men stick together when it comes to cheating!

I also got a kick out of writer Freddie Fox. He was an older man and had a great wit. Mr. Hope loved it as well. The jokes were funny and lots of them.

The same goes for Seaman Jacobs. He was another great in the business of comedy.

Doug Gamble was on the writers' list. He was young. I only say this with the caveat that I had never met him in person. On the phone he sounded like a young Doogie Howser type.

BOB HOPE'S BUNGALOW: Tales From The Typing Trenches

I can't say I knew too much about Mort Lachman other than reading some of his old jokes in the vault which were hysterical.

Tom Shadyac and Mel Shavelson were also on the list of joke meisters. I had seen their jokes in the files and knew they were funny.

If I needed to call them to get more jokes, I had all their numbers.

Chapter 20

FRANCES

Frances was the bookkeeper. She was a big mama and was a tall robust woman with steel gray hair fixed up in a large free-standing bun. It was so high up I think it had its own zip code. Fran was a no-nonsense workaholic. There was no fooling around. She was the ultimate worker and I liked her. She did smile every so often which made her more approachable. I just wanted her to like me.

"Like me. Really like me," my inner voice called out to her. For those who don't remember, these words that I just mangled, were taken from part of Sally Field's momentous acceptance speech for winning Best Actress at the Oscars in 1980.

Fran's desk was in a small office which pointed directly at my desk. She could hear every word I said. Fran handled the checkbook for Mr. Hope and paid all the bills, which I heard through the office grapevine, included a

BOB HOPE'S BUNGALOW: Tales From The Typing Trenches

bill from the Motion Picture and Television Hospital where Jerry Colonna lived out his remaining years thanks to a heart attack he suffered in 1979. Ultimately, Jerry died of kidney failure in 1986. It's a bitch getting older.

Just to refresh everyone's memory, Jerry Colonna played the zany sidekick in Bob Hope's radio shows of the 1940s and 1950s. I wish I had heard those shows but they were before my time. The two of them apparently got big laughs from the public for those radio programs.

Getting back to Fran, she was there at the office to work and had such incredible focus. She was a very capable woman with a husband. I admit, I was apprehensive of her at first. She was a big woman and could stab you with a raised eyebrow with nary a word. I really wanted her to like me so I tried to keep a low profile and stayed out of her way. However, that didn't last very long.

The only thing that bugged Fran was noise. She had to concentrate on all those numbers. From my point of view, it was a thankless job. Until I arrived, no one laughed in that office as far as I could tell. At least, they didn't laugh too loudly. It was eerily quiet for the most part except for a few quiet snickers from those typing up the jokes. Noise was not an option BCS (before Carol started).

I got on Fran's bad side when I started laughing out loud at the writers' jokes. I tried to suppress my laughter but that only made it worse. I also was a snickerer. One time, Fran actually told me to stop laughing. It broke her train of thought when she was doing the books. I tried my best not to laugh, but it was hard; rather it was darn near impossible. I'm a natural-born laugher, especially if the jokes were funny. And there wasn't any day that the jokes weren't funny. Needless to say, I got on Fran's nerves every day. Whoops.

Fran's husband had suddenly died during my time at Bob Hope's. All of us at the Bungalow wanted to comfort her. But she didn't want anyone feeling sorry for her. She was so stoic and brave.

All of the office staff drove over to attend the funeral service of Fran's late husband who was lying in the casket about to be eulogized and then buried. I had told Marie that I hated funerals and especially open-casket funerals. She assured me that this wouldn't be the case.

As we walked into the church to view the casket, I noticed that it was open. As we got closer I grabbed Marie's arm and whispered, "It's wide open. We're going to see a dead man!"

I was beside myself. Marie told me to hush. It would be all right. Don't make a scene.

As I got closer to the casket, I was shaking and started to cry. Marie put her arm around me and tried to drag me away toward the pews. I knew I was making a scene, but I was so upset. As I sat through the funeral ceremony, tears were streaming down my face. It was so sad.

Fran eventually came over and thanked us for coming. She looked at me and gave me a hug, to my surprise.

When Fran came back to work the following week, she was entirely different toward me. Maybe it was the tears over her deceased husband or the thankfulness of having the entire staff at his funeral, I'll never know.

But from that day forward, Fran was a whole lot nicer to me. I was happy. All along, I wanted her to like me and now she did. So sorry it had to be because her husband has passed, but it was like a weight had been lifted from me.

Chapter 21

BIG DOGS DO BITE

    I love dogs. But Bob Hope's two large Labrador dogs, Shadow and Snowjob, one black and one white, were considered the guard dogs of the property and were known to bite.

    Shadow was the black lab and Snowjob, or just Snow, was the white one. They were beautiful dogs but trained to guard their master and the home.

    Marie from the front desk told me the infamous story about how the dogs attacked one of the secretaries. This poor woman was bitten on her breast and her right hand. She was the secretary that the dogs trusted and loved. Both of the dogs slept under her desk. She petted them and played with them. The bad news was she went away for a vacation and when she got back I guess the dogs had presumably forgotten her or were pissed that she took time off. Go figure.

    I don't remember her name but Marie said this secretary was always playing with the dogs and loved them.

Her first day back from her vacation, the secretary went out to see the dogs over by the trees behind the Hope house. The secretary was all alone and playing with the dogs. I don't know how it all transpired but Marie said she heard screaming. The secretary had somehow got the dogs all riled up. One of them was jumping up at her and had bitten her breast. It was bleeding. The other dog joined in and she had to fend off both dogs. It must have been a frightening scene to be alone with the dogs when they were attacking her. She somehow got up and ran toward the Bungalow with blood on her blouse and her hand was bleeding profusely. Marie said her right hand was bitten several times. She sustained nerve damage which was so bad that she couldn't type. Marie and/or Nancy must have rushed to the door to call the dogs off her. The secretary stumbled in and collapsed. She had tears in her eyes and blood all over. They rushed her to the hospital where doctors performed emergency surgery on her hand.

I think her job was the one that was open when I applied to be Secretary # 2. In essence, I was stepping into her shoes at her old desk. I still shudder at the thought of those dogs jumping her. It was a good thing Nancy didn't tell me that story during my interview. I love dogs, but I sure didn't want to be the appetizer.

Initially, Bob Hope didn't want to pay for her injuries but was forced to pay for her doctor bills. Last Marie heard was that she retired to Hawaii and opened a gift shop from the cash settlement Mr. Hope gave to her.

It's no wonder I had nightmares about the horde of dogs on the property. One afternoon, I also found myself inadvertently alone with them. Talk about sweating and whistling as I tried to get away from two of them without triggering a full-fledged attack. I will never forget that day!

I had told Nancy I was going outside for a few minutes. Kathy wasn't around but Nancy and Marie said they would cover the phones.

It was a really slow day so I strolled outside to get some sunshine. I spied the deck chairs behind the Bungalow and sat down. There wasn't a cloud in the sky, just a light breeze on my face. I leaned back and closed my eyes. I could hear a lawnmower in the distance and opened my eyes. In front of me

BOB HOPE'S BUNGALOW: Tales From The Typing Trenches

were the two guard dogs, Snow and Shadow. They were circling around me. Then my eyes flew wide open. My heart was pounding as Shadow laid down beside my chair almost underneath it. Snowjob, the white dog, was sniffing the ground at my feet.

All I was thinking was, I am alone and the two guard dogs are with me, just like they had been with that other secretary. I couldn't see anything from the windows. No one was around to see if the dogs overpowered me. No people were outside. No Armando, no cooks, no masseuse, no one. I was starting to sweat profusely. My heart was pounding like a drum. I was scared. Should I get up and make a run for it? Could I run faster than the dogs? Are you kidding me? I wasn't Jackie Joyner from the Olympics! What was I going to do? I didn't want to get attacked. I didn't want the dogs to rip off my breasts and eat them for a snack. I didn't want to get blood on my clothes. But I had to get out of there. I had to get back to the Bungalow. It was a really long way to go around the Bungalow and get to the side door. Droplets of my sweat kept falling through the cracks of the wood and spilling onto Shadow, the black Lab. He made a weird sound, like he was annoyed. My only hope was to gingerly get up and walk nonchalantly back toward the Bungalow.

I got up slowly. Snowjob lifted his blond head wondering what I was up to or maybe he wanted to play. I was pretending to look around for a stick. I was even talking to myself trying to let the dogs know I was a friendly and wouldn't hurt them for the world. I secretly was praying that they couldn't sense my fear. I started to whistle and said, "Guess I'll just toddle off now." I slowly turned and moved toward the Bungalow. As I was halfway to the back, I looked inside the Bungalow. I could see Marie up front. Nancy wasn't around. I was going to rap on the windows to alert her, but thought better of it. What if I triggered the guard dogs into action? No, I was going to glide slowly toward the door. I was whistling to myself and looked down. Darn it! The dogs started to follow me! It took all of my willpower not to start running for my life. I just kept smiling at the dogs who were now both flanking me. All three of us were making our way to the door of the Bungalow. My blouse was soaked from my sweat. Snowjob kept sniffing the ground. The door was a few feet away. And then I heard a man yell, "Hey!"

I froze in my tracks. The dogs started to growl. I was a dead man, or rather, a dead woman.

The man came out of the Bungalow. It was Armando.

"Hey, what's happening?" he said to me.

"Not much. Can you get the dogs away from me?" I squeaked.

He smiled and looked at the three of us. I was the one in the middle who was sweating and about to scream. The dogs were just staring at him and looking up at me. Something was going to happen. Either I was going to faint or the dogs were going to rip my breasts off and gorge themselves. I was envisioning Armando beating them off of me with a stick. I was swaying, trying not to fall over.

Armando whistled for the dogs to follow him inside. Once they did, he threw a ball to them and they darted toward Marie's desk.

As I moved one foot in front of the other, I got to the door where Armando helped me inside. He let me sit down and catch my breath.

"What happened?" he asked.

"I was scared."

"Did the dogs bite you?"

"No, but they were poised."

He looked me over and said, "No bites?"

I started to weep and looked at him through my tears. "No, but they could have."

"Come on," he said. "You're okay. Your imagination just got the best of you, that's all."

He helped me over to my desk where I gladly was going to sit down in my chair. I stopped. Suddenly, Snowjob got up from underneath my desk and moved out of the way.

"Go in the other room, Snowjob," scolded Armando, waving him toward Fran's office.

The dog left and I literally fell into my seat.

"Do you need some water?" asked Armando, genuinely concerned.

"Yeah," I said.

Armando started to move toward the water cooler.

"And put a splash of Scotch in it, while you're at it," I said with a wan smile.

"You got it," he said and went into the other room.

When he returned with the water, there was a strong taste of alcohol which started me coughing.

"You said Scotch, but all I could find was Tequila," he winked.

"That'll do," I said taking another sip.

Armando pointed his finger at me, "No more alone time with the dogs, okay?"

I just looked at him as he did a little soft shoe out of my office and looked back with a big grin on his face. I crossed my eyes at him in jest and waved as he left. Thank God for Armando!

I started to grin.

I survived a near bloody massacre and lived to tell about it. What's next?

Chapter 22

WARD MADNESS

Ward Grant was Mr. Hope's publicist. He worked very hard because Ward was serious at his job. He was a very big man with a beard who filled up a room when he entered. It was obvious to me that he revered Mr. Hope.

No one messed with Ward because he could be fierce. Don't get me wrong. Ward also was charming and sweet when he needed to be. For the most part, he was another kind soul working at Hope Enterprises.

However, there was that one time though, that I tried his patience.

Ward knew I was great at signing a near flawless Bob Hope signature.

He called and asked me to sign the Christmas gift that Mr. Hope wanted everyone at the office to get. Ward said he wanted me to swing by after work and do the signing.

I guess I wasn't listening because all I heard was the word "signing." I didn't want to work late into the night signing a million fan mail gifts.

BOB HOPE'S BUNGALOW: Tales From The Typing Trenches

Ward begged me to stop by but I wouldn't have it. I said no. If Ward wanted me to sign anything, he would have to come over to the Bungalow on Moorpark and before 5:00 p.m.

I was a little demanding in those days.

Ward was mad but he drove over and gave me the plate to sign. All I had to do was sign the words "Bob Hope."

"That's all the signing you want me to do?" I asked. I was prepared to do more.

"That's it, my dear. Thank you," he said curtly.

Off he went back to the Hope Enterprises offices.

Ward wasn't as friendly to me thereafter. I guess I can't blame him. He had a job to do and I was being a PITA. You know, pain in the… backside. I guess he had every right to be mad at me.

Can you apologize to someone after almost four decades, or did I just get in under the wire?

Chapter 23

MY DATE WITH CHUCK

I had managed to put off my date with Chuck for months. Now I had no choice but to go through with it. As you recall, his mother, my landlady, set us up.

This begs the question, why do married couples make it their life's work to get single people married? I ask that not because I need to know, but because it's a phenomenon I've encountered many times. Some of us do not want to get saddled with a husband, house, and/or children. Yes, we do exist but are not in anyone's face so we aren't noticeable to the general public.

I was of the mind that I would find the right guy sometime during my life, but not in my twenties or thirties. I wanted to live it up a little bit first before settling down with the old ball and chain.

Which brings me back to why I was set up for a blind date by my apartment manager. The street I lived on in Glendale was lined with apartments as well as small houses. It was perfectly situated for me. My complex had an elderly couple who managed the building. Gloria and Max were their names. They were perfectly normal in a *Rosemary's Baby* (1968) way. You barely knew they were there except for the devilish goings on in the night.

Every night Gloria liked to seduce Max just to hear him make noises. It was unnerving to hear an older couple going at it. Unfortunately, the whole neighborhood heard it, too.

Gloria always tried to get any single girl hooked up with her son, Chuck. Because she was a hot mama, Gloria thought every other girl was the same as her, man hungry.

Chuck was in his late twenties and was sort of attractive, if you squinted. Not exactly my type but he seemed nice enough. He didn't have any nose rings or any garlic around his neck, so no vampires to worry about. In fact, I was willing to go out with him.

He didn't have a full-time job. I could hear him sometimes on his typewriter always pecking away. I thought he was a reporter of some kind but never really inquired.

Gloria thought we'd be perfect for each other. In actuality, she thought any single woman would be perfect for Chuck.

You know I hated being set up by a friend or a neighbor who thought they had found the perfect guy for me. It never worked out. It was a waste of time, but what do you say to that person who was only trying to do you a favor? You can't say no, can you? Maybe I was just too nice.

When I met Chuck at my door, he was dressed in a ripped Grateful Dead tee shirt and torn jeans. It was the style of the day. I didn't like it because when you go on a date, you should at least dress up a little. I was dressed in my finery and even donned a pearl necklace.

Chuck was NOT someone I wanted to be seen with. He actually looked like a bum. He had long brown thin hair which he flicked back with one hand constantly. I was tempted to loan him a barrette.

I sighed inwardly but went on the date anyway. I knew it would be a bust. But I didn't realize I was being used by Chuck to jumpstart his "career."

Chuck was nice enough but a typical know-it-all. It turned out that Chuck was obsessed with breaking into show business.

We went out to dinner at a restaurant in Glendale called Damon's Steak House on Central Avenue. Later the restaurant moved to Brand Boulevard. Damon's wasn't seedy, but it was dark and small and sexy. You barely had enough room to walk down the aisle through the darkened restaurant. If you blinked trying to find the restaurant on the street, you missed it. Damon's had Polynesian decorations, lots of tanks of fish, and Hawaiian music playing in the background. Delicious, huge steaks and Mai Tais were the draw. Lots of cops and fire fighters frequented the place. People always got loaded on the sweet Mai Tais and I attest to this personally.

Chuck paid for everything as well as the Mai Tais. I was beginning to think he liked me. But, no. He was far more interested in Bob Hope. Chuck grilled me about my job working at Bob Hope's home.

"So what do you do at his house?" asked Chuck as he tried to fit half of the steak into his tiny mouth.

He chewed with his mouth wide open. Small droplets of blood from the steak were squirting out. I tried to look away but couldn't. It was similar to coming upon a car crash where a body is in the road. You just can't look away. I was getting nauseous.

"I'm one of the secretaries," I said, still entranced with Chuck's chewing.

Chuck swallowed. Hard. I wasn't sure, but I think I saw part of the steak move down his throat. I know his Adam's apple bobbed out of the way. I was transfixed watching his throat.

"A secretary," he mused. "That means you have access to just about anything, right?" he said going in for another hunk of meat.

"No, I just type the jokes every day," I said looking beyond Chuck and seeing a dessert cart coming our way.

"Hope must have a lot of connections. I mean, he's been in the biz a long time. His rolodex must be huge," said Chuck, almost spitting at me. He added emphasis on the word, huge.

"Not as big as you think," I said nonchalantly.

The dessert cart was within reach. I had barely touched my steak.

The steak was almost raw and lay bleeding on my plate. Not very appetizing to me. I like a well-done steak. At least if it was burnt to a crisp, I knew it was dead.

"I have this script," Chuck began.

Here it comes, I thought to myself. Another wannabe wanting to become famous.

Chuck brought out the script from underneath the table. He had it in his "man bag." It must have been over five hundred pages. Chuck dropped it on the table. It was so heavy, the table almost buckled. I know some of my Mai Tai spilled out of my glass.

I looked at Chuck who was looking down at his work of art. He obviously was very pleased with it and himself. He looked up at me with those puppy dog eyes.

"It's a comedy," he said smiling and batting his eyes. Do men flirt with women like that these days, I wondered? Did I miss something when they were handing out relationships between men and women?

"Well," I started to say. "You know stars don't take unsolicited material."

"Can you get it to his agent?" asked Chuck earnestly.

"I suppose I could ask Mark, but I make no promises," I replied steadfastly.

"I'll take whatever you can do. Here you go," he said as he slid the script closer to me.

What could I do? I had to now lug this script with me.

The waiter stopped at our table with the dessert cart.

Chuck looked at it and said, "No, thanks. I'm watching my figure."

He smiled at the waiter who rolled his eyes. Then the waiter turned toward me.

I was about to say, yes please to the chocolate cake when Chuck spoke for me.

"She's not hungry. Look at her plate. The steak has barely been touched," said Chuck.

I was about to reprimand Chuck and my mouth was open, but no words came out.

The waiter shrugged and moved away.

I sat there with my mouth open, staring at Chuck.

Chuck said, "You'll thank me later," and continued chewing.

I sat back ready to scream at him.

"Waiter!" shouted Chuck to no one in particular, yet everyone in the room turned in unison and stared at us.

"Check please!" shouted Chuck even louder.

The waiter looked over at Chuck who was now snapping his fingers.

I just sort of slid down into my chair hoping no one would recognize me. I was embarrassed and couldn't wait to get out of there.

Chuck took me home and waited until I unlocked my door. He was breathing heavily. The steak undoubtedly was trying to escape from his body.

I was about to step into my apartment when Chuck grabbed my arm.

"Nice evening, right?" he said.

A smile was plastered on my face. All I could do was nod like a bobblehead.

"Let me know what happens with the script, okay?" said Chuck sweetly.

"Will do. Thanks for dinner," I said gritting my teeth as I tried to move my leg into my apartment.

Chuck leaned toward me with puckered lips and steak breath. His eyes were closed.

I was stunned and made a face and quickly turned my face so all he got was the side of my cheek.

"Night," I said as his blood-stained lips hit the side of my face. I started to close the door.

"Let me know," said Chuck, oblivious to my rejection.

I finally shut the door gently, pushing Chuck's body away from the door jamb. Through the small glass spy hole I watched Chuck move away from my apartment and sighed.

That was a turnoff, but I said I'd try to get his script read and I'm a woman of my word.

Later in the week I did ask Mark Anthony, Bob's agent, as he walked through the Bungalow.

"Do you look at unsolicited scripts to read for Mr. Hope?" I asked.

Mark stopped and looked down at me and sighed heavily. "No, my dear. We never do that."

"That's what I thought," I said ready to leave it there. Mark's answer was a NO.

"Unless," said Mark thoughtfully, crossing his arms. He always had something up his sleeve, I thought.

I looked up at him curiously.

"Unless what?" I asked.

Mark perched a butt cheek on the corner of my desk.

"Unless you wrote the script, then I'd probably look at it, as a professional courtesy," he said, wiggling his eyebrows. Whether that was true or not, I just went with it.

I cleared my throat. It was the wiggling eyebrows that got me.

"No, I've tried screenwriting," I said, "and it's too hard to impress anyone."

"If it's the right script and I liked it, then I might be able to help," he purred, leaning toward me. Was purring supposed to get me hot and bothered, I wondered? I was new to this sort of sexual exchange in an office environment.

"I kind of doubt you're going to like this one," I said.

Mark shrugged his shoulders. "Too bad. You coulda been a contender," he said in his sexy Marlon Brando voice imitating a line from the film *On the Waterfront* (1954).

There is nothing like imitating lines from a movie to get my juices flowing. I often recited the classic lines of movies myself. It was a hobby of mine.

"I prefer a happier ending, like in the 1960 movie *The Apartment*," I said to Mark in my most breathiest Marilyn Monroe voice.

"You mean the lines at the end, between Jack Lemmon and Shirley MacLaine?" asked Mark. He and I were in sync.

"Yeah, they're my absolute favorite lines," I said looking dreamily into Mark's dark brown eyes as he looked back at me. That was his cue to recite them to me.

In my mind, I felt the room closed in and began spinning as Mark recited the lines with such emotion only a great actor can muster.

"Did you hear what I said, Miss Kubelik? I absolutely adore you," breathed Mark with his one eyebrow cocked as high as he could get it.

I looked up at him through my dark eyelashes and just smiled sweetly trying to act like Shirley MacLaine from the movie. I stood up and leaned toward Mark.

As the room spun faster, I found my hand gripping onto a deck of cards. All background objects were swirling in the circle around us.

"Shut up and deal," I softly replied, holding the cards out to Mark.

Mark took the cards from me.

Our eyes met and held. All outside sounds ceased as everything swirled around us. Our hair was blown backwards as if in a windstorm. Mark's face was inches from mine. My lips were close to his as we stared into each other's eyes. My heart beat faster.

I kept staring at him as he held the cards, hoping for the impossible which never came.

"Loved that movie," Mark said quietly, wiping his eye.

The spinning slowed down as the sun filled the room. Everything went back to normal.

I sat down again trying to regain my composure.

My heart was still pounding like a drum.

As I leaned back in my chair, I thought there might have been a real tear or two in Mark's eyes as well. Darn it! I brought a man to tears! I didn't know if I liked that feeling and decided I needed to say something to him to at least smooth it out. Why am I always the bad guy when it comes to expressing my feelings?

"Mark," I said softly and reached for his hand.

But Mark had moved away toward the door leading out into the driveway. I lusted after him as the sounds of typing and phones ringing filled the air.

Those powerful lines from *The Apartment* (1960) I will never ever forget. If a guy ever said them to me in real life, I would absolutely melt into his arms.

Alternatively, I had hoped Chuck would just forget about his spec script and go away. Unfortunately, I was not that lucky with Chuck.

Chuck was always calling me for a status update on his script. Finally, I told him Bob Hope wasn't interested. He just told jokes. Scripts were out.

"What does that mean?" asked Chuck.

"I'd spell it out for you," I said sweetly, "only I can't spell."

Then I fluttered my eyelashes. I was quoting yet another line from *The Apartment*.

A dumb expression flickered across Chuck's face. He couldn't think of a comeback. Not surprised. You can't compare snappy banter by a legend like director Billy Wilder with a low-brow like Chuck.

That cooled the relationship with Chuck and myself considerably. I tried my best to avoid Chuck in the apartment complex. In fact, I avoided him like the plague. Then Chuck stopped calling me altogether.

I should have returned the script to Chuck but that would have meant seeing him again. And Chuck never asked for it back. As far as I was concerned, that chapter was shut. The key was thrown away, or so I thought, until Chuck and one of my other dates literally crashed into each other in my apartment several months down the road. But I'll go into that later.

Chapter 24

THE NEW CHRYSLER

I got a call from Mr. Hope just after 9:00 a.m. asking me to find Armando.

"Armando's running an errand for Mrs. Hope," I told him. "Is there anything I can do for you?" I asked.

"Yeah, why don't you come out of the Bungalow and meet me over at the driveway."

"Be right there," I said.

I dashed out the door into the Hope's backyard and ran over to the car parked in the driveway at the bottom of Mr. Hope's stairs.

He was already there pacing around.

"Hey, do you know anything about cars?" he asked me.

"I own a car so… maybe?" I said straight-faced. Of course I knew about cars. I had owned classics. My first was a 1965 Ford Mustang and I loved that car.

"This is a brand new Chrysler with all the bells and whistles," he said without his happy face.

"It sure is nice and shiny," I replied.

"Yeah, but I can't figure out where the horn is on the inside," said Bob. He was agitated.

"Funny. I say that to myself every morning. Where's the horn?" I quipped.

"Are you imitating me again?" he asked. Mr. Hope always thought I was imitating him one way or another. I don't know why. I never consciously did. Or maybe I was? Who knows?

"Me? No! I can't imitate you. You're the King of Comedy. Long live the King." I bowed slightly.

"God, you're really shoveling it," he smiled. "More than my writers do."

"All shoveling aside, do you want me to show you where the horn is?" I asked changing the subject. I wasn't an expert on new luxury cars.

"Yeah," he said. "Show me, Truman." That was a reference to President Truman who was from Missouri, the Show Me State.

Suppressing a smile, I went from Carol, to Hey do you know anything, to Truman, all in one morning.

I opened the door and the smell of new calf leather seats hit me. It was intoxicating. I slid in behind the wheel on the driver's side. I was short so I barely could look over the wheel. Mr. Hope was outside pointing at the instrument panel. I looked at everything and somehow hit the wipers button and the wipers toggled back and forth. Then I found the air conditioning. But where was the damn horn!

Mr. Hope looked frustrated. He couldn't see where it was either.

Then I spied it. The tiny horn insignia was off to the right hidden in plain sight. I pressed it and lo and behold the horn beeped, scaring Mr. Hope. He started grinning at me and I grinned back. Found the horn! He leaned through the open window and saw where it was exactly.

"Good job," he smiled.

I felt like a million bucks. How many people can say Bob Hope said 'good job' to their face? Just me. At least just me for today. I didn't know if he handed out words like that to everybody every day. But I felt good.

"Now promise me you'll stop telling my jokes," warned Mr. Hope.

"Even the one about politicians?" I asked.

He stopped. "Which one is that?"

I said, "It's so cold in Washington that politicians have their hands in their *own* pockets."

Mr. Hope shook his head. "Especially stop telling that one!"

"But that's your joke," I protested as I got out of the car.

"I know. But you need to give it that slow burn look at the end."

Naturally, I tried to do the look for him.

Hope looked at me. "Do you need an enema?"

"I was doing the burn," I said laughing.

"Stick to typing, kid," he said with a smile. Everyone's a critic, I thought to myself.

Mr. Hope started back up the stairway to his room.

"Tell Armando to see me when he gets back," he said and waved.

I waved back and dashed into the Bungalow with a big grin on my face. I actually told a big movie star where the horn was! It's the little things in life that make all the difference on whether it is going to be a good day or a great day.

Today was a great day for me. High five!

Chapter 25

FIRST MOBILE CAR PHONE

Bob Hope is credited for being the first person to be on a car phone. That is what his advertising executive told me.

But he was wrong. Technically, it was me that was the real first one who was on a mobile car phone. The ad man had to speak to me first because I initially answered Mr. Hope's phone. I called him on the error and the ad man from the advertising agency told me my voice would be edited out since they wanted their client, Bob Hope, to be considered the first one on a car phone. It's a small thing, but technically, I was the first, but the world will never know that unless they read this book. I haven't found anything to back up the claims about it being the first car phone but then again how many celebrities can say that they ushered in the new era of electronics in cars?

The ad agency brought out everybody to film Mr. Hope answering the phone for one of their commercials. Lights, action, camera and Mr. Hope was in his element. I think I saw the commercial a few times but that was eons ago.

I'm sure no one remembers it but me. I just want to say, it was *my* 15 minutes of fame. No drums, no fanfare, no lights. And that's the way I like to shine, with no one watching. It was just a footnote in history. Okay, it was really just a comma.

Chapter 26

BIG TYPE TYPEWRITER

Bob Hope had an eye disease which as he got older made it hard for him to read the large cue cards which had his jokes printed on them. These visual aids used at a live event or during a TV special were invaluable to Mr. Hope. I believe he was one of the first to use cue cards. Each time the writers fed their jokes of the day to me, I ran them upstairs to Mr. Hope who tinkered with them, rearranged them and finally got the jokes to the way he wanted to deliver them to the audience. After that, he called down to the secretaries to have the cue card guy print them as large as he could onto the big cue cards. The cue cards had to be enormous since Bob had to read them from the stage.

One time I had to use the Big Type Typewriter that was custom made for Mr. Hope's needs due to his eye problems. It was like printing on the Gutenberg press. Everything was like a typewriter only five times the size. Enormous! Each press I made on each large key was like swinging an axe down as hard as you could by using one finger. In other words, it was akin to slamming down a sledgehammer for each letter using your fingertip.

I finally got everything typed and gathered up all the sheets of the letters, and brought them up to Mr. Hope's room.

"I've got some revised jokes. Let me find them so you can type them up," he said and began to rummage through everything on his desk. He couldn't find the pages and looked everywhere including under the bed.

The door to his bedroom from inside the house was locked.

I heard Mrs. Hope saying something to him from inside the house. She rattled the locked door but Bob was oblivious to her. He was looking for his revised pages that he wanted to give to me to retype. I could hear her asking him to unlock the door.

Either Mr. Hope didn't hear her, or he chose not to hear her. Sometimes people do that if they're annoyed. At any rate, he never went to his door to let her in.

"Ah ha!" he said. He found the pages under the bedcovers.

"Here you go. Call me when you've finished typing them," said Mr. Hope and guided me toward his outer door leading to the steps outside.

By this time Mrs. Hope was pounding furiously on his door. She wanted in!

He said thanks to me and went to his inner door and opened it. I could hear Mrs. Hope angrily asking him why he didn't open the door for her.

Mr. Hope said he didn't hear her and then went about memorizing the new jokes on his desk.

I think she was pissed but I couldn't see her face.

I ran down the steps quickly. I didn't want Mrs. Hope to think I was eavesdropping on them, which I wasn't.

Sometimes wives get weird and it's best not to be within eyeshot, or earshot, if you know what I mean.

Chapter 27

TRAPPED AT THE POOL

I was casually taking a stroll around Bob Hope's property on my fifteen minute lunch break and came across the back of the Mansion where the pool was. What a magnificent view! The closely-cropped grass was never ending. There were flowers blooming everywhere and if you looked out of the two-story house, it was a spectacular view. I usually was on the other side of the house on the blacktop driveway leading up to Mr. Hope's bedroom.

As I walked over to the pool, I saw Armando in full sight and waved to him.

"So this is where you hang out," I said to him.

"Nice pool, isn't it?" said Armando with a grin.

"Nice? You mean this gorgeous lake? Yes, it is fabulous."

"Mr. Hope has good taste," he said.

"I'll say. I never knew he was *this* rich," I replied.

"Shhh, Mrs. Hope might hear you," warned Armando in a whisper.

"Oh yeah, she rules the roost, right?"

"She IS the roost!" said Armando with a grin.

"Well, I better get out of here before she sees me," I said backing away, right into the portable grill knocking it almost off its foundation. The sound was what frightened me the most. Both Armando and I froze when we heard Mrs. Hope's voice ring out. Cue the music from *Jaws* (1975).

"What on earth are you doing, Armando!" yelled Mrs. Hope.

Armando gave me that OMG look with raised eyebrows. He looked like he had been caught with his hand in the cookie jar again and was terribly afraid. I guess Mrs. Hope could scare the dickens out of anyone. Marie had told me that in confidence. Now I know what she meant. I was scared not only for Armando, but for myself. I wasn't supposed to be out by the pool goofing off, even though it was my lunch break.

We could hear Mrs. Hope coming, like the shark in *Jaws* (1975). I darted around, and frantically tried to find a place to hide among the deck chairs. Armando was doing the same thing. I slipped behind one of the potted plants and backed up against the wall and waited. Armando wasn't so lucky. He was in the line of fire.

Mrs. Hope had thrown open the sliding glass door and yelled over to him, "I see you, Armando! Come over here!"

The whites of Armando's eyes were bulging out, but he turned toward the sound of her voice behind the sliding glass doors.

"Yes, Mrs. Hope?" he said nervously.

"Did you knock over that barbecue grill?" she asked.

"That grill over there?"

"No, the neighbor's next door," she replied sarcastically.

"I might have bumped into it," he said, swallowing hard.

"You've got to be more careful, Armando," she chided.

"Yes, ma'am," he said, looking down and over at me.

"Put the grill back in its place and then you can go," Mrs. Hope said.

Armando straightened up the grill as Mrs. Hope had requested and then he gave me the evil eye.

I just stood there like a statue with bug eyes, unable to move. God knows what Mrs. Hope would have done to me. Tar and feathers perhaps?

"I'm going now, Mrs. Hope," said Armando loudly.

"Be careful on the freeway. I hear it's a full moon tonight," she said.

Armando nodded and darted off.

I was still trapped. Mrs. Hope would not leave that damn window. How was I going to get out of there, I wondered.

Then, without warning, I heard the sound of claws clicking across the patio stone. The dogs raced through the pool area. I'm sure they smelled me, or was it my fear? But there they were, Snowjob and Shadow, standing directly in front of me almost poised like pointer dogs. Holy Mackerel, they were unnerving.

I tried to shoo them away but they just stood there frozen in time. What did they want? I didn't have any treats. Maybe they thought *I* was the treat. To tell you the truth, I was more than a little scared. I couldn't stay hidden behind the pot and yet I couldn't move away. I was trapped!

By now Mrs. Hope was wondering what was going on with the dogs.

She stepped outside and looked over at them. Both dogs turned toward her on cue and growled. I was praying they wouldn't bite her like they did everyone else. Mrs. Hope had the same fear and backed up. She looked worried.

Suddenly Armando appeared giving Mrs. Hope a start. She had her hand over her heart.

"Do you want me to put the dogs in the Bungalow?" he asked as he moved toward them.

"Yes, that would be a good idea," said Mrs. Hope breathing heavily. She went back inside, presumably for a cocktail. I could have used one myself!

Armando took the dogs away while still watching me.

As I moved from the potted plant, I tripped over the pole that was used to catch leaves in the pool and landed flat on my face. My nylons were torn and my knees were scraped. How many ways can you spell klutz? What else could possibly happen to me, I wondered as I lay there afraid to move.

Armando let out a high-pitched whistle to the gardeners working out on the grassy knoll. One of them came rushing over to me and helped me up. We went all around the Hope house and back to the tar driveway to avoid Mrs. Hope's evil eye. I thanked him profusely and then walked toward the Bungalow and quickly slipped inside.

Inside the Bungalow, I saw Armando and raced over to him

"Do you think she saw me?" I whispered. I didn't want anyone to hear us.

"She would have had a fit if she did," he replied, also in a conspiratorial whisper.

Kathy was in the back and saw us talking with our heads together. She suspiciously looked at my bloodied nylons which were split open at the knees. Kathy gave me the once over and said, "You were gone over an hour."

"I'll make up the time," I said.

The phone rang and Kathy reached for it. Mr. Hope wanted her upstairs asap. She gathered up her pen and notebook.

"I'll be with Mr. Hope for a while. No more falling down, okay?" she said indicating my bloody knees and then rushed out of the Bungalow and up the driveway to Mr. Hope's room.

Fran had heard and seen everything and looked at me questioningly. I wasn't about to tell her where I had been.

"I tripped," was all I said. Well, it was the truth!

Fran shrugged and shut her door. She had work to do.

As I pulled out my chair, the two dogs that were hiding under my desk flew up and out of the way, nearly knocking me over. That was the last straw, because one minute I was standing on the floor, and the next I had jumped up Ninja-style onto my desk crouching and holding my stapler as a weapon. The dogs and I were at war! They were barking up a storm when Marie came back to my desk. Then I felt the room start to spin. When I came to, I was on the floor and Marie was hovering over me fanning me with a sheet of typing paper.

"I knew sooner or later I'd have to talk you off the ledge," she said shaking her head.

That night the nightmares started and I dreamed about those darn dogs for months!

Chapter 28

THE DEN

I would always sit in the den in the Bungalow if I wanted to get away from the phones or have a quick bite of lunch. The den was used as Bob Hope's extra office outside of his two-story house. It served as a catch-all for the trophies, trinkets, and gifts from the G.I.'s from World War II. It was dark and gloomy inside. It reminded me of a stuffy warehouse filled with memorabilia.

I usually sat at his huge wooden desk and ate my bag lunch that I brought from home. There was no going out to a restaurant for lunch. That is why my hours were 9:00 a.m. to 5:00 p.m. That time frame was eight full hours of work with a quick bite of 15 minutes to eat for lunch. I didn't mind. I had nowhere to go and tons of work.

What was interesting about the den were the items I saw on the desk and shelves. There was an actual machine gun on top of the tall cabinet behind

BOB HOPE'S BUNGALOW: TALES FROM THE TYPING TRENCHES

Mr. Hope's desk. One military man had given that to Mr. Hope as a "trophy." It was scary to me. Wasn't it illegal to own a machine gun in the suburbs? It was out of reach so it actually didn't present any danger.

I was looking for a pen inside the drawers of the desk and saw a bunch of black and white photographs. There was a still scene of dead people lying in mass graves. I presumed they were Jewish people that had been killed by Hitler's army. It was an eerie photo which still is atrocious today as it was when it was taken. As I rifled through the rest of the pictures of the dead, I was struck with an overwhelming feeling of sadness. Those people didn't deserve to die. They were just innocent people in the wrong place at the wrong time. I shut the drawer quickly holding back the past and my tears.

As I ate my sandwich, I noticed a far more cheerier picture of an older Bob Hope standing next to a young Tom Selleck in a Hawaiian shirt. As I looked at the Polaroid, I smiled. Tom was a tall, good-looking man. It must have been taken around the time of his *Magnum P.I.*, (1980) days or shortly thereafter.

I finished my sandwich and walked past a statue of a huge golden Oscar in the corner of the room. It made me laugh because I remember that Academy Award show where Bob Hope was the host and continually made light of the fact that he had never won an Academy Award. That year the Academy "gifted" him this award. I believe one of his opening jokes was "Welcome to the Academy Awards, or as it's known at my house, Passover."

I wondered how Bob got the statue home from the Academy Awards show that night. It was huge and probably needed a crane to move it. But there the giant Oscar statue stood in the corner of Mr. Hope's den in all of its glory like King Tut's buried coffin waiting for the world to rediscover it.

Chapter 29

THE UNDERWORLD

The phone rang again. This time I knew the caller's voice.

It was Mark Anthony, Mr. Hope's agent. Cue the song from *The Godfather* (1972).

Mark was an attractive man. Not old in any respect, but he must have been in his fifties. Slick dark hair, mustache, about six-foot tall, well-dressed always, and his persona seemed a little bit over the top. Let's just say, I would have hated to meet him in a dark alley. There was something dangerous about him and I'm not referring to the fact that he was an agent. Something was bubbling close to the surface. Perhaps anger, something intense, something explosive you didn't want to get near. Mafia? I never asked. I had seen the movie *The Godfather* over a decade ago and that was enough for me. I specifically went out of my way to avoid Mark. I could have been wrong about him. He could have been teaching Sunday school in a church basement somewhere,

BOB HOPE'S BUNGALOW: Tales From The Typing Trenches

but I doubt it. There was just something a little bit off, and I didn't want to find out what it was.

As I explained to Mark, who was on the phone with me, the one and only Milton Berle was already on the phone talking to Mr. Hope.

Mark said, "Okay, have Bob call me back. No, on second thought, I'll just drive over." Then he hung up. I looked down at the dead receiver in my hand. Does anyone in Hollywood ever just say goodbye, I wondered as I replaced the receiver back in its place on the phone's cradle.

I already had Mark's name written on the message pad with his phone number since he usually called in quite often.

Mark Anthony was an agent who had worked for Mr. Hope for years. He knew everyone and everybody in the business. He had seen it all. Rumor had it, Mark was connected to very dangerous people, but no one could prove it or even wanted to broach the subject. But he had that scary persona similar to the tough characters found in films about the Mafia. People who were so focused they were able to destroy things without blinking an eye. Mark was a dark, brooding, threatening figure who wielded this kind of power and who ruled the land of the Bungalow in Toluca Lake where Bob Hope lived. Mark was the maestro of Bob's career but lived in the dark underbelly of Hollywood, chewing on cigars, making deals and piloting careers. Those that didn't believe in the power of talent agents were in for a shock. It's the agents that broker most of the deals, good and bad, for the entertainers and actors, et al. Mark was a master at it. He was a killer agent who was tough, smart, and deadly when he had to be and no one crossed him. But to think he was some sort of hitman for the Mafia which Marie had inferred? I don't think so. Then again, what did I really know? I was just the secretary. I was an outsider.

Bob Hope was in Vaudeville back in the 1920s. Sixty years later, are we supposed to believe Bob was associating with hitmen? This was Bob Hope, and Mark was not the Bogeyman!

Marie buzzed me and whispered into the phone that she saw Mark in the driveway and to get ready for him and his "entourage." I didn't know what she was talking about because I didn't think I had to "get ready" for Mark. But I squared my shoulders and patiently waited at my desk for his cameo appearance. I really wasn't expecting anything out of the ordinary. Was I surprised!

I was sitting alone at my desk when Mark Anthony and two other men were ushered in by a stone-faced Marie. She was not her bubbly self as she led the three of them back to me. I looked up and recognized Mark and smiled at him. When I glanced over to take in the other two men, I froze. My eyes honed in on the two men and my blood ran cold down my spine. Were they out of Central Casting? Let me explain. The only way I can describe these two men is that both of them appeared to have no necks. That in itself was frightening. Both were in identical camel coats, dark shirts, and these guys were big and burly with football shoulders. There was no expression from either of them. I actually did wonder if they were supposed to look like killers or they just needed an enema that morning. Prunes, anyone? They wore black-mirrored sunglasses. They had short-cropped old-style dark hair. They were swarthy-skinned. Could they be the Mafia? Did Mark bring the Mafia into the Bungalow? To Bob Hope's house? I was scared. Did they have guns underneath those camel coats? Or worse, were they machine guns? By now I was sweating. Where was a weapon in the Bungalow? A hammer? In a pinch, I thought I could use my stapler, or better yet, my tape dispenser. It had a rough zig-zagged edge, but it was hard to hold. I doubt I could toss it and make contact with anyone. Okay, I know I was overreacting but I was a high-strung chick and worried about the crime wave going on in 1983. My adrenaline was pumping.

All three of these characters stood at my desk, in a horizontal line, not smiling, just waiting for me to call and announce their arrival to Mr. Hope. It was weird. My heart was pounding. I took in a deep breath to steady my nerves. I let out a ragged breath. I was shaking.

I quickly turned to the phone, knocking it completely off its pedestal. To be honest, I get a little klutzy in times of crisis. As the phone slammed to the ground, the receiver bounced off sliding across the black and white floor. Now I had to retrieve the receiver while they stood over me. None of the men moved a muscle to help me, those bastards. I was embarrassed, mainly because I had on this very short skirt and for those women who have been there, it is very hard to bend over in a tight short skirt without showing a little skin. I had to slowly sink down to the floor on my haunches and pull the phone by its curlicue cord up and toward me. If I bent too far over, my derriere would be exposed for everyone to get a good shot of it. No pun intended. I crouched down and yanked the receiver part with the curlicue cord and it sling-shotted with full force toward me. The phone's mouthpiece came flying at me and now it was a missile which almost hit my mouth. I fiddled around with this phone for a full minute because it kept bouncing around with the curlicue cord that was attached to the base. Finally, I was able to stand up with the phone and nonchalantly walked around my desk to sit down. It was nothing I hadn't done a million times. You do this crouching curtsy, grab whatever you have dropped, and slowly move upwards with your precious cargo, all in one fell swoop. It was a ballerina-like movement.

Not one of the three men moved a muscle. No one cracked a smile. All six of the eyeballs of the men bore into me. I was just a tad flustered as they watched me. I swear four of the eyeballs were reptile-like. Their eyes were narrow and flicked from side to side. I give Mark a pass since he was one of the Hope "friendlies." Not that he was overly friendly. To clarify, he was NOT. But at least he was a humanoid and still had a freaking neck!

I nervously dialed Mr. Hope's number and let out a croak to announce, "Mark Anthony is here with two other, uh, people. Mark said you were expecting them?" I said to Mr. Hope, more in the form of a question.

"Oh yeah. Send them up," said Bob into the phone and hung up.

I looked at Mark and said, "Go ahead. He's waiting for you and your, uh, friends."

Mark threw me that agent look of superiority and almost sneered at me. He was attractive, as far as agents go, but I really hated that look of "I'm so much better than you, doll."

As the last burly no-neck "hitman" passed by my desk, he gave me a wink. Shocked, I sat up ramrod straight and did a double take. He was softly whistling as he and the other two waddled out of the room. Did that hitman actually wink? At me? Good grief! My head was spinning off its axis.

As the three of them lumbered off up the driveway leading toward Mr. Hope's bedroom, I glanced over at Marie at the front.

She also had been watching them and shook her head. I took that look as "Yes, they are the Mafia and they're here in Toluca Lake! Run for your life!"

The pictures behind me on the wall were of Italians and churches. They were a gentle reminder that you could not owe a debt to powerful people without having to someday pay it back. An offer no one could ever refuse. I learned that from Mario Puzo's book *The Godfather* (1972).

I finished out my shift and waited around, but Mark and his two neckless buddies never came back downstairs.

That night I prayed Mr. Hope would be okay. I had seen the movie *The Godfather* (1972) and hoped that Mr. Hope's fate wasn't on the same track. In other words, I hoped there would not be a horse's head lying next to Mr. Hope in his bed.

Chapter 30

LUCY

I remember Lucille Ball called Bob one day and I could not have been more nervous. Lucy was my idol. Her antics were hilarious on screen. Yes, I admit it. I was starstruck by her.

"I've got to talk to Bob, right away," she said into the phone in her deep, husky voice.

"Yes, Miss Ball. Please hold on," I said almost jumping out of my seat.

I knew Lucy's voice immediately so I didn't have to ask who it was.

After all, Lucy was the Queen of Comedy.

If there's a funny face or a pratfall to be had, Lucy did it. She didn't care that she looked ridiculous. She was darn funny. She acted like the rest of us, the dumb and the dumber. If you could wring a joke out of a skit where you picked up chocolates from a conveyor belt and stuffed them in your mouth until your mouth was ready to explode, she did it. That skit was a classic.

In the skit Ethel and Lucy are working a conveyor belt where the chocolates move along the belt. They are supposed to be picked up and put into boxes, but the belt starts to go faster and faster with Lucy and Ethel stuffing chocolates into their mouths to prevent a back-up of the chocolates from falling onto the floor. The faster the belt went, the more chocolates were stuffed in their mouths until they looked like squirrels with cheeks bulging out to infinity.

Lucy's facial expressions had me laughing and on the floor. It was like watching an egg-eating contest and the person is beyond full. There is no more room to fit in one more egg, let alone swallow it. You knew that at some point the person was just going to heave up the kitchen sink, eggs and all. Why we, the public, take such joy in this "sport," go figure. Maybe we're happy they'll do it or we just want to see the person squirm.

If you watch classic TV, you will find Lucy's skit. It was and *is* hilarious.

I chuckled to myself as I put the real Lucy on hold and got Mr. Hope on the other line. Then I jiggled the receiver to connect the two of them. I could hear both of them laughing and trying to top each other with a joke. Reluctantly, I released the call. No chocolates for me.

Chapter 31

SHIRLEY TEMPLE BLACK

I was sitting in Nancy's chair talking to Marie when a call came in. I answered it with my usual deep throated, "Hello."

"This is Shirley Temple Black. Is Bob available?" she asked rather sweetly.

My mouth dropped open as soon as she said Shirley Temple, and all I could think of was the tune, "On the Good Ship Lollipop," sung by a young Shirley Temple.

As some of you remember, Shirley Temple was the little girl who danced and sang her little heart out in the old film *Bright Eyes* (1934). She was the number one box office draw as a child entertainer from 1934 to 1938. Everyone loved her! I hadn't been born but she was so famous in the thirties. Later in life she became a businesswoman and diplomat. She ultimately died in 2014.

When Shirley Temple called in asking for Mr. Hope, I pulled myself together and said in my usual secretarial tone, "Mr. Hope is not available right now but could I have him return the call?"

Shirley was so cordial and friendly.

She said, "Of course."

Then she asked, "Are you new? I don't recognize your voice."

I told her I had replaced another secretary and this was my first time working for Mr. Hope.

We chatted a bit about Mr. Hope and how much she enjoyed his joke telling. I felt like a trusted girlfriend. It was like talking to an old friend. I had watched all the old movies and enjoyed the ones when she was just a kid.

I told her she was so young when she started and I was amazed that she got out of Hollywood unscathed. She laughed and said she was amazed, too. Then she talked about the movie industry in the early days and Vaudeville and Bob Hope. All of this was years before I had been born, but I sure enjoyed speaking to her. Back then when you are an Ambassador for the country, that's big news. The bonus was speaking to Shirley Temple. Double big news. Shirley was just what the world thought of her. She was a sweetheart and a lady.

Here are just a few of her diplomat credentials that she had amassed as an adult:

1974 to 1976 she was Ambassador to Ghana.

July 1, 1976 to January 21, 1977 she served as Chief of Protocol of the United States.

1989 to 1992 she was Ambassador to Czechoslovakia.

Chapter 32

BEACH BOY MIKE LOVE

No matter how you slice it, The Beach Boys are Americana. I grew up listening to their surfer music like "Wouldn't It Be Nice," "I Get Around," "God Only Knows," "Sloop John B.," "Help Me Rhonda," "California Girls," "In My Room," "Don't Worry Baby," "Be True to Your School," "Little Deuce Coup," and "Little Surfer Girl." There are more songs too numerous to list, but you see how many songs they sang. The Beach Boys were legendary, especially to Baby Boomers. Hello, that would be me!

At that time, the Secretary of the Interior, James Watt, became one of the most controversial cabinet appointments made by President Reagan. Watt had banned rock bands from the National Mall in Washington because they attracted "the wrong element." He wanted a wholesome element like Wayne Newton. These so-called dangerous bands included The Beach Boys. Everyone from The Beach Boys themselves to Nancy Reagan was outraged by

Watt's comments. Because Watt didn't want The Beach Boys, Wayne Newton eventually got the National Mall gig. However, the publicity bolstered The Beach Boys' career because they were booked by everyone else! White House staffers awarded Watt a plaster foot with a hole in it signifying that Watt had symbolically shot himself in the foot.

It wasn't long before Mike Love of The Beach Boys called the Bungalow for Bob Hope.

Mike was one of the original co-founders along with his cousins Brian, Dennis and Carl Wilson, and friend Al Jardine.

When I picked up the phone, the caller said, "Hi, it's Mike Love from The Beach Boys."

My mind flipped and I heard in my head their 1966 song, "Wouldn't It Be Nice" by The Beach Boys.

Suddenly I'm on my feet pointing at Marie who was walking by.

"It's The Beach Boys!" I whispered.

Yes, I was in love with their music and was thrilled to be speaking to Mike Love.

Marie smiled and just shrugged. It was no big deal to her.

Mike and I started laughing about the Watt incident which we thought was a joke. Watt didn't know a rock band from a hole in the ground. All the music Watt was interested in was "The Star Spangled Banner" and "Amazing Grace." It was unbelievable, especially in the 1980s, that the Establishment, which included Mr. Watt, was still so critical and/or afraid of the youth of the day and lumped them all together with psychedelic music to surf music. Crazy!

Imagine banning The Beach Boys from the Mall. You can't get more patriotic with music when you listen to a Beach Boys tune.

Isn't that right, Little Surfer Girl?

Chapter 33

DOROTHY LAMOUR

On another call I was treated to hearing Dorothy Lamour asking me if I could get an autographed picture of Bob Hope for her.

Dorothy Lamour had acted with Bob Hope and Bing Crosby in the Road pictures and she was a constant in their pictures. These movies were a combination of comedic romance, adventure and plenty of gags. They were comedic satires on the film genres of the day.

These are the seven Road pictures:

The Road to Singapore (1940).

The Road to Zanzibar (1941).

The Road to Morocco (1942).

The Road to Utopia (1946).

The Road to Rio (1947).

The Road to Bali (1952).

The Road to Hong Kong (1962).

Dorothy was the original sarong girl which meant she usually wore a sarong when the three of them were on a beach somewhere cooking up jokes and shenanigans galore. These "*Road to*" movies came out in the 1940s with the same cast and always involved a crazy storyline for the three of them which delighted most of America. The movies were all comedies and satirized the film genres of the day such as Arabian nights, the jungle, the high seas, and so on.

I told Dorothy I would make it my mission to get an autographed picture of Bob for her collection and I did. All I had to do was put an unsigned picture on the pile of mail with a request that Dorothy Lamour wanted him to personally sign it. He laughed, as usual. The three of them had been friends for years!

"And now she wants my autograph?" he chuckled.

I could have signed it for Dorothy, but it wouldn't have the same meaning as Bob's real signature.

When I called Dorothy and told her I got the autographed picture, she was thrilled to pieces. I had made her day, which made my day.

I was sad to hear she died in 1996, but I still have these fond memories of her.

Chapter 34

HALLOWEEN

Halloween was a strange one that year. I believe Mr. Hope was out of town doing a "smoker" and Mrs. Hope was not in the house. I was alone with the security guard catching up on some filing when the night closed in around us. It was around 5:00 p.m. We could hear the Trick or Treaters out on Moorpark Street running from house to house squealing.

Three kids actually walked up Mr. Hope's driveway and stood outside the double Dutch door singing the famous words, "Trick or Treat." I had some wrapped chocolate-covered candy pieces in my purse. There was enough for the three kids. I opened the top of the Dutch door and looked out.

There they were, looking up at me: a ghost, a black cat, and an orange pumpkin. Their costumes were delightful and their faces were all smiles. The little girl was the black cat and her two front teeth were missing. She was small for her size but spunky. The two boys were about nine years old and flanked the little girl.

"Aren't you kids adorable," I said to them as they held out white pillow cases for their treats.

I put a handful of candy into each pillow case as the kids squealed with delight.

"Can we see Bob Hope?" asked the pumpkin all wide-eyed and hopeful.

"Please, please," yelled the other two, jumping up and down.

"Bob Hope isn't home," I said sadly.

"Can we see his house?" pleaded the black cat. "Please?"

The kids were so excited to look at a celebrity's house.

I looked over at the security guard who was shaking his head, no.

Ignoring him, I unlocked the Dutch door and let them inside.

"I can show you the pool area, but that's all," I said.

All three of them cheered and jumped up and down again. I put on my best sad face and looked at the guard pleading with him to let me do this for the kids.

The security guard looked glum. He didn't want to ruin their Halloween either.

"I'll get the dogs and put them in one of the rooms for a few minutes," he said against his better judgment and went outside to whistle for Snowjob and Shadow.

As the guard brought in the dogs, he put them inside one of the nearby rooms and locked the door.

"The coast's clear," he said to me. "Be quick."

I took the kids' small hands in mine and we walked outside. The third child, the pumpkin, was holding hands with the black cat.

The Hope house was dark. Only the lights from the pool area were glistening in the night.

As the four of us strode over toward the pool, we passed the small golf course area with a sand trap off to the side. I saw the pool up ahead behind the house. There were a few Halloween decorations here and there. The glistening pool water looked beautiful with lights set up along the edges that flickered on and off. The kids *oohed* and *aahed*. They were entranced. We stood there for a minute and then I saw fireworks of differing colors exploding in the night sky.

"Look up, kids," I said, pointing up at the sky.

All three kids looked up in unison.

Fireworks were popping from some unknown place in the distance and made everything magical for the kids.

Every firework was different in color and size. The kids were thrilled and let out more *oohs* and *aahs*.

Suddenly, I heard a door slam loudly.

The security guard came running outside toward us. He was obviously frightened.

"You've got to get these kids out of here," stammered the guard. "She's back!"

The guard had his hand on his heart and was trying to catch his breath.

I looked toward the gate. Was it rattling? My eyes widened.

Mrs. Hope's car had stopped outside the gate and was honking. Cue the music to *Jaws* (1975).

Throwing up his arms in fear, the guard ran back to the Bungalow to attend to the gate.

I pulled the three kids with me toward the Bungalow. I was afraid! We raced past the golf area, but the pumpkin fell. I jerked my head to the left because I heard the gate slowly trying to creak open. The four of us were not out of harm's way. The pumpkin had started to roll toward the side of the hole and I chased after it with the cat's and the ghost's hands in both of mine. We must have looked like something out of *The Wizard of Oz* (1939) as we raced after the pumpkin.

By now the winds had kicked up and everything started to blow every which way. The black cat's tail had snapped off and was airborne. It landed in the pool.

I pulled the kids with me toward the Bungalow. We had a hard time moving forward into the raging winds.

The guard was also having problems with the gate. I could hear gears grinding, but the gate just wouldn't swing open.

As the kids and I got to the door of the Bungalow, I turned my head and looked back at the Hope house and did a double take.

The house looked like it had white wispy air squeezing out through every opening!

Then it dawned on me. It was the night of Halloween! We all knew the Hope house was haunted. Could that wispy air be "ghosts" flying out of the house like bats escaping from hell and flying directly at us?

Then everything went pitch black.

The electricity had gone out in the neighborhood.

No one dared to move. I felt for my gold cross around my neck and held it up trying to ward away any devilish spirits.

Suddenly, a firework in the distance exploded and a vision of an angel appeared and hovered in the sky. Was that an omen?

I grabbed all three of the kids and pushed them inside the Bungalow.

The guard pole-vaulted over his desk and got us into the den and locked the door on us.

Mrs. Hope's horn was still blaring outside the gate. You didn't have to be a genius to know she was pissed, especially now that it had started to rain.

As the guard dealt with her, the kids and I huddled together on the floor in the dark den. I comforted the kids telling them everything was going to be okay. We heard rain pelting the roof.

There was a gigantic clap of thunder making everyone, including myself, scream out loud.

Then as fast as the storm came in, it was gone.

Still no lights, but the rain had stopped. The kids felt safe.

How exciting this Halloween had been for them and yours truly!

The kids got up, now that their fears had disappeared, and explored the den. I kept shushing them because the last thing I wanted was Mrs. Hope to hear them. I doubted if she could, but you never knew what a hearing aid could pick up, if she had one.

The kids were enamored with Mr. Hope's huge golden Academy Awards Oscar in the corner and were touching it.

The guard gently knocked on the den's door.

"It's safe to come out," he said through the door. I could hear him unlock the door.

"Where's Mrs. Hope?" I asked the guard.

"When the electricity came back on, the gate opened and she just drove in," he replied.

The three kids and I emerged from the den. I got my purse and the four of us walked out through the Dutch door. I was still holding the kids' hands as I escorted them to the sidewalk.

"Thank you, Mrs. Hope," they squealed in delight and walked down the street with some other trick or treaters who were passing by.

"*Mrs. Hope?*" I repeated. Did I look like I was that old? Wait a minute. Kids always thought anyone over thirty was old.

All that really mattered was that the kids had a good time at Halloween, even if it scared them out of their wits.

Chapter 35

DEADLINE AND DOGS

I remember when Mr. Hope wanted all the writers to come to the Bungalow to write new material. My job was to call all of them to come over. They showed up at the Bungalow ready to come up with a bunch of new jokes. These guys took over the little spare room that no one used and barricaded themselves inside. Nothing like a room full of gag writers trying to outdo each other. The laughs from the spare room came fast and furious. Not my laughs, but theirs. They were tossing around jokes left and right trying to top the next person. It was hysterical.

Bob Hope gave them a deadline of forty-five minutes to come up with fresh material.

Meanwhile, I was in the office with Marie, Nancy and Frances. We were doing our own jobs. I left my desk to get some water to drink while Nancy brought in the two guard dogs that were outside.

BOB HOPE'S BUNGALOW: Tales From The Typing Trenches

The dogs had to be in our area so that the writers could go outside and up the driveway to present their jokes to Mr. Hope.

Robert peeked out of the door of the spare room, where the writers were, and motioned for me to come over. He wanted me to type up the jokes they had chicken-scratched on paper so far. Then he froze. He saw the dogs pacing around behind me.

"What are they doing here?" he hissed.

Robert was a survivor of several infamous dog bites at the Bungalow and never ever turned his back on the dogs.

"They're inside until you guys leave," I said.

Robert gave me the handwritten jokes and quickly went back inside the spare room, shutting the door firmly. The spare room was filled with nine or ten writers so it was a tad cramped to say the least.

I returned to my desk and typed up everything. Robert called me on the phone and said they needed whatever I had because Bob Hope wanted them upstairs asap. I gave him all the jokes and the writers started to file out of the room.

The phone on my desk rang. It was Mr. Hope wanting to know why the writers weren't upstairs in his room. At the same time Marie had transferred another call to the phone on the desk situated behind her, which was for Robert. She told Robert there was a personal call for him and to pick up the phone on the spare desk, which he did. Then she got distracted by another phone call that came in.

While all this was going on, Shadow the dog, crept up behind Robert. He was facing the wall and leaning over the spare desk talking on the phone. As I turned my head in Robert's direction, I saw the dog was near Robert's butt. Then I heard a blood-curdling yell ring out. Everyone froze. Shadow had just bitten Robert in the butt drawing blood. It happened so fast no one could have anticipated it. Robert should have, because in 20/20 hindsight, he knew the dogs were going to get him sooner or later. I guess he had one of those butts that was just too tempting for the dogs.

Nancy was fast and ran over and grabbed the dog and dragged him to another location in the Bungalow before anything else more deadly could happen. Robert, while cursing because he was in pain, limped over to the spare office holding his butt, presumably to wipe away the blood that was starting to spread on the back of his pants.

I was so caught off guard that the only assistance I could offer was to give Robert a band-aid, but it was a mini, which means it was the size of my pinkie. I'm sorry, but that's all I had!

Robert looked at me and then at the tiny band-aid.

Then he said, and I'm paraphrasing, "Really? That's the biggest band-aid there is? In this million dollar estate, this is the only size you've got!"

I felt bad and sheepishly shrugged and just backed away.

No telling who was going to get bit in the butt next.

Chapter 36

MORE DOG BITES

Speaking of dog bites, another veteran of the teeth-baring dogs was the writer, Martha Bolton, the first female staff writer who I believe started around the same time as I did.

I don't know why I am the person who witnessed these chompings, but for some reason the dog, Snowjob, was lurking around in the Bungalow that day. Snowjob had been under my desk when Martha came into the office. She was dropping off jokes for Mr. Hope. She stood over me and we chatted for a minute. Martha had to get back to her husband who was waiting outside in the car.

I got up and walked with her toward the door. We were laughing. Martha was walking next to me on the right. Snowjob was on the left side of me. Quickly the dog crossed behind me to the right and then I heard a "sniff" sound. As soon as we passed by the spare desk up front which was behind

Marie's desk, I heard a combination growl and a bark. I can't quite describe it, but Martha stopped dead in her tracks.

"Are you okay?" I asked her.

She obviously was in shock.

"I don't know," she said and rubbed her foot.

"I think the dog just bit me," she said, no longer smiling.

I was stunned, yet again.

"Snowjob bit you?" I asked, looking down at Martha's foot.

Martha held up her hand that had touched the top of her foot. It was bloody.

Marie jumped up and got Snowjob outside as fast as she could.

"Do you want to sit down?" I asked Martha.

"No, my husband is waiting," she replied.

"Do you want to go to the hospital?" I asked.

"Yes, I'll have him take me there," she nodded.

Martha hobbled over to the door, blood still on the floor. She beckoned for her husband who got out of his car.

Marie came inside and she and I helped Martha into the arms of her husband. He got her into his car and they went directly to the local hospital.

"Where's Snowjob?" I asked Marie.

"Outside," she replied.

I had to tell Mr. Hope about the incident but he didn't seem too upset. He made a joke about his writers giving their all for him, including blood. He smiled at me but I knew he wasn't kidding.

Later I heard Mr. Hope paid for Martha's dog bite, as opposed to last time when he was threatened with a lawsuit by a former secretary if he didn't pay for her dog injuries.

Chapter 37

JOHN RITTER

One celebrity that impressed me was John Ritter. He called to speak to Bob Hope about one of Mr. Hope's specials but Bob was on another call.

As usual the phone rang around 9:30 a.m. and I answered in my usual husky voice.

"Hello," I said.

"Hi, is Bob there? It's John Ritter," said the caller.

I loved John Ritter. He was such a natural comedian and actor on the sitcom *Three's Company* (1977).

"I'm sorry. Mr. Hope is on a long distance call. Can I have him call you back?" I said.

"I suppose," replied John.

There was a pause. I felt like he just wanted to talk.

"Is there anything else I can help you with?" I asked.

"How are you?" he asked me.

I stopped. Did I hear him correctly? Did he really ask how I was? No one ever stopped to inquire about me. Ever! It was rather refreshing. I turned away from Frances and looked out the back window.

"Right now I'm feeling fabulous. I'm looking out the window at Mr. Hope's beautiful green lawn. It goes on forever," I gushed.

"I heard he has a really beautiful estate," said John.

"The best. Toluca Lake is a great place to live. You know the area, right?" I asked.

"Oh yes."

There was another pause.

"Are you okay?" I asked, finally breaking the silence.

I was wondering why he wanted to shoot the breeze with me.

"No, I'm fine. Really fine," he said.

"I love *Three's Company*," I said trying to change the subject.

"Thank you. It is a cute sitcom, isn't it?" he said.

"Thanks to your comedic talent," I mused.

I wasn't kidding. John Ritter was great at comedy.

"That's nice to hear," he said humbly.

"I'm sure Mr. Hope will call you right back," I offered.

"That will be great," he said. "Enjoy the sunshine."

"Thanks, Mr. Ritter. I'll be seeing you on the boob tube," I laughed.

"It's John," he corrected me. "Mr. Ritter was my dad."

"Got it," I replied. "Have a good day, John," I said brightly, even though I wanted to talk to him longer.

We hung up. I felt there was something going on with him or maybe he just was that way with everyone. Being friendly with secretaries doesn't happen that often, so I was glad to banter back and forth with him.

Little did I know that John Ritter would eventually pass away from a heart issue similar to mine at St. Joseph's Hospital in Burbank on September 11, 2003.

I always thought John was one of the nicest guys in Hollywood.

Chapter 38

DAVID SOUL

If you are old enough, you'll know who David Soul is from his TV series *Starsky & Hutch* (1975-1979). He was very cute and had a headful of gorgeous blond hair. I suppose since the *Starsky* character had dark hair, the producers wanted a distinct contrast between the two of them. Thus, David Soul was the blond male lead.

David and Bob Hope worked together on one of Bob Hope's TV specials and became friends. For some reason Bob had great affection for David Soul. Let me explain.

At Christmas time Bob always sent gifts to his family and friends and the worker bees.

That Christmas in 1983, Bob sent David Soul the biggest and best gift basket of all.

Marie commented, "Why is David Soul getting the best of the fruit baskets? Wonder what he did for Mr. Hope."

"Maybe he bought Mr. Hope a gift that was so generous that Mr. Hope had to top him," I suggested.

Marie snorted.

"No, everyone knows Mr. Hope is rich because he holds on so tightly to his money," she joked.

"Yeah, I wish we could have hot chocolate at least at Christmas time," I said like one of the Dickens' children. "Can I have more, please, sir?" I mimicked.

Marie smiled and shook her head.

I had no idea at the time, but Mr. Hope was not known to be a big spender on those around him. In fact, it was well documented, that he was cheap.

Everyone was jealous. David Soul got the best of the best of the fruit baskets, and the rest of us got plastic clocks signed, not by Bob Hope, but by me! I had to forge Bob Hope's name on the plaque's clock face.

Then that part had to be glued onto a piece of clear plastic where a small round clock face was placed into the plastic frame. The inscription read "Merry Christmas from Bob Hope."

In Mr. Hope's defense, those that went through the Great Depression, which started in 1929 and ended in 1939, were extremely careful in guarding their money, even years later. Bob Hope, Jack Benny, and the late great *Tonight Show* host, Johnny Carson, were notorious cheapskates. Bob and Jack were around during the Depression. Johnny had been born in 1925 and the Depression left its mark on him as well.

Chapter 39

ELIZABETH TAYLOR

Liz Taylor had quietly checked into Betty Ford for rehab. No one knew she was there. But Bob did. One late afternoon he called and told me to get Liz on the phone.

As everyone knows, Elizabeth Taylor was a very famous and beautiful actress. She started in the forties as a child actress in *National Velvet* (1944), and was extremely well known in the fifties where she won the Best Actress Award at the Academy Awards show for the famous movie *Butterfield 8* (1960). She was known as a businesswoman for the Passion and White Diamonds perfumes in collaboration with Elizabeth Arden, Inc., and as a humanitarian as co-founder of the American Foundation for AIDS Research. All in all, she had seven husbands, not all at once. That would be a lot of men to juggle!

As I was flipping through telephone pages for Liz's home number, Bob said, "She's at Betty Ford."

That was a name I had heard of before. Lots of famous and not so famous people went there to "detox."

"I'll get her for you right away," I said.

"Just tell them Bob Hope wants to talk to her," he said like I would be able to part the Red Sea and get Liz on the phone. No, this was going to be tricky.

I got the number for the Betty Ford Institute and dialed.

A nurse came on the line and I asked to speak to Elizabeth Taylor.

The nurse hesitated.

"I'm calling for Bob Hope," I said.

She stalled and pretended she didn't know the name.

"You can check with Miss Taylor. She's waiting for Mr. Hope's call," I said, totally lying.

"Hold on," the nurse finally said.

I was on hold close to ten minutes. I assume they were talking to Liz. If she didn't get on the phone, I would have a lot of "splaining" to do as Ricky Ricardo would say.

Finally, the nurse came back on the line and put me through to Liz.

"Miss Taylor? Bob Hope is calling," I said almost too perkily. I'm sure she was in withdrawal.

"Oh, yes of course," she said in a husky voice in her very best English accent.

I jiggled the line to put Liz on hold and got Bob on the other end and jiggled the line again. They were connected. I could hear them talking to each other.

Both were very glad to speak to one another and that's when I disconnected myself from the three-way call. I would have loved to hear what they said but it was private and I respected that.

One final note, although Liz was tireless in her fight against AIDS, she ultimately died of congestive heart failure in 2011.

Chapter 40

PHYLLIS DILLER

Phyllis Diller was a very funny stand-up comedienne known for her eccentric stage persona, self-deprecating humor, wild blonde hair, and baggy, garish clothing, and an over-the-top cackle of laughter.

She made fun of her lack of sex appeal while brandishing an extremely long black cigarette holder with a wooden cigarette embedded at the end. She played comedy clubs and was on several TV shows. Her husband, Fang, was always included in her stand-up routine of jokes. She became a household name and influenced the likes of Joan Rivers, Roseanne Barr, and Ellen DeGeneres.

Phyllis Diller's mentor was Bob Hope. She appeared with him in several films including *Boy, Did I Get a Wrong Number!* (1966), *Eight on the Lam* (1967), and *The Private Navy of Sgt. O'Farrell* (1968).

In 1966 she accompanied Mr. Hope and his USO troupe to Vietnam where I assume the soldiers loved her humor.

I remember her calling Mr. Hope at his home.

She would just say, "It's Phyllis for Bob," in that throaty deep voice of hers, and then end with a nasal laugh that sounded like "ah hah."

The "ah hah" sound could be described as a cross between the sound of a nasal cough and the last gasp of a witch's cackle. Whatever it was, it was a Phyllis Diller classic ending.

Of course I knew who Phyllis was immediately and put her through to Mr. Hope. There was no guessing when she spoke. She had this deep, earthy voice with a little twang to it. I had heard her routines so many times and she never failed to disappoint. Her main bit was making fun of herself. I laughed out loud at her humor, knowing full well it was just an "act." No one dresses like she did. She was memorable. The way she tore into herself before anyone else could, she had me doubled over in laughter. I had never heard this type of laughter before from a female comedienne.

Phyllis Diller was one of the top female comediennes (along with Lucy) that I can remember, prior to Joan Rivers, Roseanne Barr, and Ellen DeGeneres. Phyllis certainly stood out in the crowd. How can you not, when you hear that exaggerated cackle of laughter? Sadly, she passed away in 2012 of heart failure.

I'll never forget Phyllis Diller's memorable sense of humor with lines like, "Housework can't kill you, but why take a chance?"

As well as this pearl of wisdom which really cracked me up, "You know you're old when someone compliments you on your alligator shoes, and you're barefoot."

She was one of a kind. I really loved her sense of humor.

Chapter 41

MARY HART

Entertainment Tonight reporter Mary Hart had an appointment to interview Bob Hope at his home. He wasn't quite ready for her so she hung out down at the Bungalow with us. While she was waiting, Mary struck up a friendly conversation with me. We discovered that both of us came from Minnesota and we reminisced about our time back in the frozen tundra. Minnesota was really cold in the winter time. It was almost as bad as my home town, Winnipeg.

I asked if Mary ever went to the Quarterback Club in downtown Minneapolis. It was a trendy bar catering to the Vikings football players, and others, located near where I worked as a legal secretary to Thomas Crosby, Jr., a lawyer at the law firm of Faegre & Benson. Mary said she had heard of the Quarterback Club but had not been there. Mary and I chatted about other things for quite a while and then Mr. Hope called. He was ready for Mary and her team to start filming the interview with him for *Entertainment Tonight* (1981-present).

I was so impressed with Mary's down-to-earth attitude, as well as her beauty and poise for someone in her early thirties. Yet, she was incredibly kind and friendly toward me. I wasn't the Head Secretary, only Secretary # 2. How many reporters are so beautiful, inside and out?

Later, I heard she married the film and television producer Burt Sugarman, and had a dream marriage. What a lucky girl, I thought. But she worked really hard and deserved to reap the rewards. I hope she is still living the good life today.

Chapter 42

AUTOGRAPH TIME

Speaking of autographs, I was quite good at signing Mr. Hope's name. I signed pictures, books, wood, game pieces, anything that a postman can carry in a letter or package. I practiced for hours on end until I was satisfied that my signing the Bob Hope name looked exactly like Bob Hope's signature. I was pleased that the other people in the office thought it was a darn near perfect replica. Add forgery to my list of accomplishments.

Marie had signed a lot of autographs for the fans and one time one of the items was a book about Mr. Hope.

A week later, the book came back to Marie with a note from an outraged fan.

"That is NOT Bob Hope's signature. I want the real deal!" shouted the note, or words to that effect.

Marie marched back to my desk and said to please re-sign the book and then she ripped out the cover page with the flawed signature. I was shocked she was so dramatic, but I signed a new page with the Bob Hope signature. It was flawless. Marie showed it to Frances who looked over at me and said, with a raised eyebrow of concern, "Don't come near Mr. Hope's checkbook. He'll freak." Maybe she didn't use the word "freak" because she was reserved and very proper. I used the word, because I liked to use it.

Although Frances had told me she was afraid to let me near the checkbook, she ultimately slipped one day and jokingly told Mr. Hope that I was the great forger of his signature.

Right after that conversation, Mr. Hope came downstairs to the office and wanted to see my work.

"I hear you're the best forger we have in the office," he said.

"Yes, no one can tell my signature from yours," I said half-kidding.

"That's what I'm afraid of," he grinned. "Let's see what you've got."

I took some paper and signed his name with a flourish. *Ta da*! Mr. Hope examined it closely. I think he whipped out a jeweler's eyepiece from his pocket so he could compare the forged name with his own.

Without looking up or missing a beat, he yelled out to Frances who was behind a closed door, "Fran! Keep Carol away from the checkbook!"

I heard her muffled voice reply, "You got it, Mr. Hope."

He looked over at me accusingly. I smiled lopsided at him hoping I wasn't fired.

"I've got my eye on you, kid," he said jokingly.

Bob Hope gave me a wink before he left and took the signed picture with him.

But he was still smiling, so that was a good thing.

I sighed, I still had a job!

Chapter 43

HOLLYWOOD AFTER DARK

Kathy, the Head Secretary # 1, and I were invited to attend a club in Hollywood on a Thursday night. The man who invited us even had a chauffeur lined up and the three of us drove to the Rainbow Room in West Hollywood. His name was Bill or Ted or something innocuous like that. To protect this innocent man, let's just call him Bill.

I'm sure Bill wanted something from Bob Hope and thought entertaining Bob's two secretaries would be his golden ticket. Little did he know, that was the kiss of death.

All I knew was that Bill was a really fast talker. Could it be that he was from New York? Perhaps, or maybe he was just nervous around powerful women like Kathy and myself. That was a joke. We didn't have any power at all! The most power I had was to get Armando to take me to lunch. He was always up for that. Kathy, on the other hand, I'm not so sure of. She was quiet yet managed to worm her way into various events. Not me. I was a little shy and stayed in the background. Personally, I felt at ease in a friendly environment and kept a low profile. The limelight was not the least bit attractive to me, at the time.

In Hollywood, when Kathy and I got out of the limo, Bill raced up to the bouncers at the door and announced to them and other club people that we were Bob Hope's personal secretaries. Bill kept shouting it out loud for anyone to hear. I was a little embarrassed. Why would anyone be interested in the two of us? Secretaries? Good grief, I was not glamorous and Kathy was a lot older than me. We didn't have anything to offer, other than the ear of Bob Hope. Actually, only Kathy had his ear. She typed his personal letters to his celebrity friends and the like. I was just Secretary # 2 who was like a backup to Secretary # 1. In other words, I was completely earless.

Regardless of the situation with the bouncers, Kathy and I embraced the situation and drank the night away with Bill inside the Rainbow Room.

The place was packed and he was trying to impress us with his knowledge of the Hollywood scene. Maybe Kathy was impressed. I wasn't. Bill was nice looking but he was a wannabe, in the worst way. Maybe he was Mr. Big back in New York, but not here in Los Angeles.

Finally, since all I was doing was drinking the night away, I was getting a little loaded and a lot bored. I wasn't interested in Bill and a dull night lay ahead of me like one big, gaping yawn. I got up just as a song blasted through the airwaves. It was Michael Jackson's song "Beat It." How can you NOT get up and dance to that?

I was possessed. I had to dance. I was the only one in the room spinning around and dancing with myself. I felt like I was a superstar entertaining the troops as I danced to this song with wild abandon. I don't think there was a "designated" dance area, so I made my own.

A cute guy from the crowd joined me and we were dancing in sync.

And as usually happens, more people started to get in the groove and got up out of their seats. Soon the floor was packed with everyone moving to the song, "Maniac" by Michael Sembello from the film *Flashdance* (1983).

BOB HOPE'S BUNGALOW: TALES FROM THE TYPING TRENCHES

You didn't need a partner to dance with. It was just like the old times in my apartment. *She's a Maniac. Maniac on the floor. And she's dancing like she's never danced before.* I could go on, but you get the picture.

Finally, after the next song, "All Night Long" by Lionel Richie, I went back to the table where Bill and Kathy were deep in discussion. I announced it was way late and I had to get home. I had to be at work the next day. Bill called for another limo driver to drive me back to the Hope residence so I could get my car. Kathy stayed with Bill. I guess she had a good time. She never said a word about it the next day and I never asked how it went.

Kathy really enjoyed being the center of attention and I understood that. There weren't any other perks to working for Bob. No big bonuses, no attending his shows, no free coffee in the office either. For all I could tell, being Bob Hope's secretary was just like working for a regular businessman who had a number of gag writers stuffed in his pockets. As I said repeatedly, these writers had a way with words that blew me under the table with their sense of humor. If I remember anything about the writers, it was the jokes they came up with. They were off-the-cuff, burst-out-laughing, knee-slapping jokes by a group of humorous men and women who worked for a famous, funny comedian. Can it get any better than that?

I had heard stories of Frank Sinatra flying his secretary on his private jet all over the country. That was not the case at the Hope house. It was just a secretarial job. Nine to five with your lunch break at your desk or in the den. Not exactly the job I envisioned. I wasn't anyone, just a glorified typist and occasional autograph signer. Okay, delete the word glorified.

Kathy managed to get away, though. She liked to go over to Jonathan Winters' home in Toluca Lake and schmooze with him. She also went to Mr. Hope's tapings. She was with the "in crowd" and so it wasn't just a secretarial job for her.

However, because of the stress of working very long hours, she started to feel sickly. It would have been hard to come into the office and be upbeat every day when you felt sick. She was allowed a certain amount of sick time and she took it. I was doing double duty at the office while she was at home recovering, but I loved the job so much that I didn't care. Unfortunately, because Kathy was out sick so long, the decision was made that she didn't need to come back.

Mr. Hope wanted a full-time Secretary # 1 who would be at his bidding 24/7. I still was Secretary # 2 and did my usual duties. Nancy was looking for a replacement for Secretary # 1 who would be on call any day of the week, at any time. It was an impossible task. I think Mr. Hope just wanted someone around at night so he could try out new material or just schmooze with. He wanted an older Gal Friday. I was in my early thirties and Bob's wife, Mrs. Hope, insisted on someone much older for Mr. Hope. Young chicks were out. I really don't know how I got through the gray curtain. Everyone was at least in their mid-forties or fifties. It was a staff of elders. Perhaps it was because Bob Hope came from Vaudeville and was in his eighties, or maybe it was Mrs. Hope who wanted older women who wouldn't fool around with Mr. Hope. I can only speculate. Mrs. Hope was a bit jealous of the flirtations of the young. I didn't consider being thirty as young, but I was the youngest person on staff in the Bungalow. Listening to jokes all day was definitely fun, but I could see I couldn't go any further up the "corporate ladder" because there wasn't a ladder, not even a step stool.

One day I was the only secretary left in the Bungalow. I still was Secretary # 2. The downside was the job was low paying, working for an eighty-year-old, and with no chance of advancement.

When I tried to invest in my apartment that had gone condo, the mortgage agent laughed and told me I didn't make enough money to own my own place. I was stunned.

Here I was, working for a millionaire comedian, yet I didn't make enough money to buy a cheap condo in Glendale. Perhaps I needed that kick in the pants to move forward.

At any rate, my new mission was to start making more money. I had no choice, I had to give my notice to Bob Hope, and soon. I was sure there would be many new secretarial replacements waiting in the wings.

At least I could say I had a fun job for a while that left me laughing every single day. It was sad to leave such a fun place, but I knew I needed to go somewhere else to make big money, and lots of it.

Chapter 44

SEX ON THE BEACH

My girlfriends and I were out on the town one Saturday night doing our usual bar hopping along Wilshire Boulevard. Truth be told we were headed up Wilshire toward the Beverly Hills area. There were lots of guys and fun bars to stop in for a few drinks and see if we could stir up some fun. The name of the game was man hunting. We all were looking for a boyfriend or seeing a movie star on Wilshire or the Sunset Strip. It didn't matter where, we were just a bunch of girls who wanted to have fun, like the Cyndi Lauper song.

We stopped at a hotel bar along mid-Wilshire which looked promising. There were tons of people coming and going. I noticed that the men were good-looking and smiling so we parked the car and went into the bar. There was lots of music and the drinks were flowing.

We all were drinking Sex on the Beach, the drink of the evening, at the hotel bar. The cute man who was standing next to me started up a conversation and kept buying all of us drinks. I can only tolerate two or three of Sex on the Beach and then I'm drunk. Long story short, I found out that the man was an undercover cop called Jimmy. His main objective of the night was to try and bust a prostitution ring that operated out of the hotel. He said he knew I was a "good" girl and just wanted to sit with me while I was his "beard." To define "beard," I simply meant I covered for him as his date. He wasn't gay, just pretending to be my date so he could arrest the prostitute.

The cop Jimmy collared the prostitute and hauled her out of the bar. I finished my drink alone. I was bored, so my friends and I went to another bar further into Beverly Hills.

The place was a popular bar where a Rock Hudson lookalike sauntered over to me with a drink and handed me his hotel key. I didn't know what to do with it and stared up at him. He was very tall and had been drinking for a while.

"Please come by later tonight and meet me in my room," he murmured.

I stared into those dark brown eyes and couldn't believe he said that to me.

People were crowded all around us. It was like midnight in New York City just before the New Year rang in.

That guy was so blatant, I thought to myself. It was kind of an insult. Did he think I was a prostitute?

"Rock" downed his drink and drifted away as the crowd closed in. I fought my way over to the bar where my friends were.

"Cute guy," said one of the girls indicating "Rock" as he was moving toward the door.

"Did he get your number?" asked the girl.

"No, but I got his," I said looking down at the key in my hand.

I ordered a drink and then went to the ladies room.

An older woman attendant was cleaning up the towels and wiping down the counter. I handed her a tip. After all, she had a tough job. She smiled at me before she left.

I saw the empty trash bin and started debating with myself. Did he really expect me to go to his room? No way! That's when I tossed the key into the trash bin.

The Rock-Hudson-looking guy was beyond handsome, but God knows what would have happened. He could have been Rock Hudson, or not. I wasn't prepared to find out because I wasn't a famous person, and I certainly didn't want to sleep with a famous person. What future could there be in that?

Chapter 45

THE PENTHOUSE SPREAD

Just for the record, I am not a connoisseur of *Playboy* magazine or of *Penthouse* magazine, which was more "hard core," but when the news broke that Miss America had done a naughty spread for *Penthouse*, it was really big news.

Mr. Hope was on the phones with many people trying to track down a copy of *Penthouse*. It was the biggest news of the day since the Miss America Pageant was so squeaky clean.

When Vanessa Williams, a beautiful black woman, won the title of Miss America, everyone was thrilled for her. But she had also posed for *Penthouse* a few years before, alongside another woman. Their pictures in the magazine at that time weren't that racy, but they were not what the Miss America Pageant would approve of for their future Miss America. Pictures of two women in compromising poses would not make the Bible Belt happy.

I finally saw the pictures after Mr. Hope and his cronies had thoroughly examined them in depth up in his room. The pictures were somewhat suggestive I guess you could say, but just by a smidge.

Everyone was a critic in those days. I thought women's rights were farther along, but I was wrong. Even in 2022, they are still not as far along as we had hoped they would be.

My job at the Hope house was to just file those *Penthouse* pictures under Miss America. It was quite a scandal. If you judged them by today's standards, people would yawn. Some say sex isn't that big of a deal anymore.

Miss America may have lost her crown, but she triumphed anyway and went on to become a star.

My observation of the whole thing was that it was much ado about nothing. Everyone back in the day liked to make a mountain out of a mole hill. Especially the men.

Chapter 46

FAN MAIL

I liked answering the fan mail. People from all over the country had something they wanted Mr. Hope to sign. I'm sure the postman had a bad back from hauling in all the mail every day.

In the early years, Bob had signed his own fan mail but now he needed a team to do it for him. He was eighty years old and had eye problems.

There were tons of letters in the mail, and it seemed like every envelope contained some sort of 3D item that the fans wanted signed personally by Bob Hope. I saw chess pieces to carved wood. You name it, the fans mailed it in, hoping that Mr. Hope would personally sign it.

I remember a beautiful, colorfully-drawn picture of a cute dog coming in and that the fan wanted Mr. Hope to name it for her. I sent back a short letter from Mr. Hope saying that the animal could be named Bartholomew, or Bart, for short. She later sent a reply back to Mr. Hope saying it was the perfect name.

How sweet of her to respond. A lot of Mr. Hope's fans were absolutely the best and they adored him.

The trouble was, Mr. Hope was a very busy man and he was in his eighties. Every night he flew out on a private plane provided by the billionaire Alex Spanos. Mr. Hope had jokes to memorize, agents, publicists, ad men wanting him to be in commercials, and anything else you can imagine. For his age, he was the hardest-working man in show business.

I am amazed he could keep up the pace which, by my calculations, went on for sixty plus years.

Who works that hard at eighty years of age? No wonder Bob Hope was still popular with his fans all over the world.

Chapter 47

THE DREAMY SERGEANT

Mr. Hope was especially popular among the servicemen and servicewomen of the Armed Forces. They couldn't get enough of him and his humor. He had earned a special place in their hearts. Mr. Hope would do anything to get on a stage, in any country, at any venue. He absolutely loved to tell jokes for them.

Bob especially liked performing for the servicemen and servicewomen stationed in Vietnam. He would go anywhere to tell a joke and always got laughs. They were literally a captive audience.

One of the writers told me he thought that Bob wanted to go out entertaining the troops. This, I understood to mean, he was willing to be put in harm's way, telling jokes in a military war zone for our servicemen and servicewomen. I agreed. That would be a hell of a way to end a career as a comedian. But, that would never happen because Mr. Hope was guarded by security. No one ever wanted him to die on their watch.

I had an interesting experience with a serviceman who wanted to have Mr. Hope donate some items to a military charity event in San Diego.

That morning I slowly drove over to the Hope house with my car radio blaring the song "Jessie's Girl" by Rick Springfield. It was a catchy tune that I actually could sing along with. I was admiring the green lawns of the Toluca Lake neighborhood in which Rick Springfield lived. Maybe miraculously he'd appear throwing his door wide open and picking up the paper or something. Then he'd see me in my car with the windows rolled down and his music spewing out. Wishful thinking. I never saw anybody but the gardeners out on the lawns. They would actually wave to me as I drove by. I smiled and waved back. I felt it was going to be a very dry summer for me.

Many gardeners were tending to the lawns of the upscale area. Mowers were cutting grass, rakes were raking the cut grass. The air was filled with the sweet smell of summer. It seemed as if everyone had a Spanish gardener working for them. The smell of freshly-cut grass of the lawns was ambrosia to me. It reminded me of Winnipeg. Big, wide-open spaces covered with grass and trees everywhere. Winnipeg is a nice place to visit in the summer. In the winter you needed snowshoes, wool socks, gloves or mittens or both, and a wool scarf to cover your face and forehead, and a snow shovel to dig out from the heavy snow drifts.

In my sunny California apartment, I had woken up late that morning and had raced around the apartment, hopping into clothes, getting dressed and trying to grab a piece of toast. I tried to drag a comb through my hair but it was almost impossible. I just had time to throw on a little makeup. My damned hair. It was the bane of my existence. I thought I would just do a quick touch up of water and try to make the curls a little straighter when I got to work. At least I never saw too many people at the Hope Bungalow, so what would it matter if I breezed in and stopped in the bathroom to try and straighten and pull my curls into place. I'd only be a minute.

As my green Firebird squealed into the parking area at Mr. Hope's, I almost hit Armando, scaring him. I waved apologetically to him. He was silently praying to the Virgin Mary as he went inside. Poor Armando was surrounded by bad drivers. I looked in my rear view mirror. My hair was beyond help and no matter how many times I spat into my fingers and tried to make it straighter by pulling on the curl, it just wouldn't unwind. The song, "Jessie's Girl" by Rick Springfield was still blaring. I hated to turn off the car, but it was 8:59 a.m. and I knew I had to walk through the door at 9:00 a.m. sharp. I turned off the car and Rick Springfield's voice just stopped. Everything was quiet. I tried to pull down a few curls onto my forehead as I opened the car door, but my hair just wouldn't cooperate. Frustrated, I slapped my hair silly. Nothing worked. Relax, I told myself. It's just going to be a bad hair day. I let out a deep breath of air and gave up. I got out of the car, still a little perturbed.

I rushed over to the front door about to go in, just as Nancy threw open the Dutch door. This was highly unusual. Nancy never met me at the door before. Something was up.

"There's someone here to see you," she said urgently and indicated my desk in the back room.

I raised my eyebrows and looked beyond her. There was someone back there but I didn't know who it was. As I cautiously walked toward him, it was apparent that this person was the tallest man I had ever seen. He was a giant and very, very cute. Cuter than cute. He was handsome; in fact, a real heartthrob. I was speechless. My mouth was hanging open, as usual.

He smiled and introduced himself as an Army Sergeant of some sort from San Diego. All I can remember thinking was what a hunk and oh my God, my hair! My ugly hair! And I can't just pop into the bathroom. What would he think? He was still smiling and towering over me and looking down and talking to me. I finally heard what he was asking. He wanted me to have Bob Hope sign a piece of memorabilia he was holding. I just kept looking at those luscious lips flapping in the breeze. Not sure what else he had to say because he was the most gorgeous man alive! Not that I was man hungry, but I do appreciate a fine cut of meat, I mean, man. I mean he was well-trimmed. I mean, he was trim! Good grief, even now I'm trembling at his beauty. Yes folks, men can be beautiful. Take it from me. I have gazed out over many men and I pride myself in knowing the difference between attractive, cute, and beautiful versus there is no way in Hell that I'd go out with him!

When the Sergeant had finished his spiel, he handed me the object he wanted Mr. Hope to sign. All I could do was smile up at him and bob my head up and down in agreement, knowing full well that I would move Heaven and Earth to get Mr. Hope to sign the object for this beautiful guy. Holy cow, I was a pile of melted putty as I stared up into those gorgeous baby blue eyes of the Sergeant.

The Sergeant thanked me and said he'd call to arrange for the pickup of the charity item. As the Sergeant walked away, I watched every muscle in his body. Okay, I looked at his butt. What a man! He turned and waved and I melted again. I smiled and waved back and then he was gone.

Marie looked back at me with her usual smirk. I think even she was impressed!

I looked at the item in my hand and then walked into the bathroom and let out a little yelp. My reflection in the mirror frightened even me! My hair was a freaking ugly sight to behold! I would have been better off if I had just shaved my head. At least I wouldn't look like an electrocuted Cabbage Patch doll!

I put the object on a nearby chair and then went to work on my hair. I struggled to straighten it with water but nothing worked. I had yanked a fistful of hair almost out by the root. Finally I emerged from the bathroom. My hair was quite wet and I could feel the so-called curls shrinking back up on my head. What a mess I was and my head had started to bleed from the yanked-out hair. Somebody shoot me, I thought as I stomped over to my desk.

The phone started ringing and I answered it with a very deep, "Hello." I went to work typing up more new jokes. I wondered if I could get my hair professionally straightened by a local hairdresser.

When I brought the jokes up to Mr. Hope's room, I asked him if he wouldn't mind signing the object the Sergeant had given me to auction off.

BOB HOPE'S BUNGALOW: Tales From The Typing Trenches

Mr. Hope was pleased they wanted his autograph and he signed it right away with a smile.

When I got back to my desk with the signed trophy, I knew I had to make sure I would be presentable for the next time the dreamy Sergeant made a return visit for his charity item.

Maybe I could cajole him into going for lunch! Fat chance.

Chapter 48

MRS. HOPE VISITS THE POPE

Mrs. Hope was a devout Catholic. She was *so* Catholic you would have thought Dolores was jockeying to replace Mother Teresa on the Pope's Greatest Hits List. If she did, she would become Saint Dolores of Toluca Lake. Dolores revered the Pope in Italy and made plans with her sister to visit him and get his blessing. All good Catholics have this hidden wish to meet with the Pope. I did, too. Can you imagine *me* getting a blessing from the Pope? Only in my dreams.

Mrs. Hope and her sister brought tons of film to Italy to memorialize the moment they met with the Pope. I, on the other hand, hate having my picture taken and would avoid a camera at all costs. Not Mrs. Hope. No matter how old she got, she loved to be photographed. I say this just as a personal observation of the woman. I wish I had her fearlessness.

BOB HOPE'S BUNGALOW: TALES FROM THE TYPING TRENCHES

I hope the Pope heard their confessions while they were in Italy. Everybody has sins and I'm sure they had their own share of sins. Or maybe not. I confess to you, I didn't know Mrs. Hope very well. I did know she wouldn't allow any fraternizing with Mr. Hope and that the staff had to refer to Bob as MR. HOPE. No one could ever call him Bob. We could only address him as Mr. Hope. This phrase has carried over with me for years. I can't just say the word, Bob. To me, he will always be Mr. Hope.

Meanwhile, since Dolores and her sister were off in Vatican City in Italy, that meant Bob Hope was free to do as he pleased at the house in Toluca Lake. It was akin to letting the prisoners run amuck for a few days. Pandemonium!

Shall I point out the obvious? The women in Toluca Lake, and the neighboring City of Burbank, were not safe!

That warning went double for the pedestrians on the streets! If Mr. Hope had a secret rendezvous at night, he drove himself around, and you remember how great a driver he was, according to Armando.

Chapter 49

THE OTHER WOMAN

It wasn't often that I stayed late at the office, but this one particular day I had a lot of work on my plate, so I decided to stay late for an hour or two. No one was around in the Bungalow except me and the security guard.

The night security guard showed up as usual and waved to me when he came in. The guard was in his sixties and I believe he had retired from the police department. He was on duty all night and generally his job was to contact Mr. Hope if anyone stopped by to meet with him. The guard had a direct line to Mr. Hope's room and would call up to announce who was at the door or gate.

That particular evening Mr. Hope had been off the property. He returned around eight. The guard yelled out to me in the back room that he saw Mr. Hope driving up to the gate. I was preparing to leave myself and walked over

BOB HOPE'S BUNGALOW: Tales From The Typing Trenches

to the guard's office area overlooking the driveway just as Mr. Hope stopped at the gate. Mr. Hope had bad eyesight and could only see the guard. I ducked down and listened in to their conversation. I was quiet as a mouse and it was dark inside the office area.

I heard Mr. Hope tell the guard to get the gate open as fast as he could.

The guard did as directed and then frantically motioned for me to see what he was seeing inside Mr. Hope's car as he waited for the gate to fully open.

I moved to the guard's area and leaned over to see Mr. Hope's car outside.

Mr. Hope was suspiciously looking around as he tried to straighten out a piece of furry material on the passenger's floor.

The guard nudged me. He indicated with his head that I should look inside the car.

I casually looked over into Mr. Hope's car, and then I saw it.

My eyes literally bugged out of my head!

Several phrases came to mind: HOLY COW! NO WAY!

And my personal favorite: Are you KIDDING me?

Bob was trying to get the furry material over the leg of a woman lying on the floor on the passenger side.

I looked at the guard who flashed me a look of amusement and then he just shrugged.

Outside Mr. Hope started to say something to the guard about how cold it was getting and could the guard speed up the gate.

Even though the guard kept pressing the open button, the gate swung so slowly that I could have gone out for a ham sandwich and been back in time for the gate to come to a stop in Mr. Hope's driveway. Once the gate was open, Mr. Hope hit the accelerator and the car jumped forward with a little high-pitched chirp sound.

The guard closed the gate behind Mr. Hope and looked at me with a lopsided grin.

"Eighty isn't looking so bad anymore," he said.

"I couldn't help but smile at him.

I had to get home and not worry about the other woman. She could have been there to share some hot cocoa with him. Whether or not, I really didn't care. Mr. Hope was still America's funnyman.

The guard held the Dutch door open to let me out.

He said, "Drive safe. And don't pick up any strangers."

What else is there to do but be safe, I thought to myself. I would never pick up anybody unless they were bleeding or were in desperate need of assistance.

"Always do. Have a nice night," I said and walked over to my car.

I thought, what a sad statement. A thirty-three-year-old woman was going home to an empty apartment and a TV dinner and my eighty-year-old boss was at home having way more fun. What was wrong with this picture?

I told myself I had to get to get a life. Yes, I wanted a boyfriend and maybe even more than that.

I promised myself that weekend I was going to make it happen.

Little did I know, I was about to cross paths with the devil!

Chapter 50

SAVED FROM THE NIGHT STALKER

I decided to go dancing with my girlfriends Saturday night. Our usual dance place was at the Holiday Inn in Glendale. It wasn't too far from my apartment and there were lots of guys from the hotel and the Glendale area who frequented the bar. I ordered my usual Scotch and water. A man who was seated got up and bumped my hand just as I was about to take a sip. The drink went flying and I lost it all when it landed on the floor. The man apologized and quickly left. I signaled the waitress for another drink and sat down in the man's empty seat. I felt a body on the other side of me. He was facing the crowd like he was looking for someone. As he turned, he caught sight of me and leaned in.

"Can I buy you a drink?" he asked in a low voice.

His face was swarthy and pockmarked. Not that I judge a book by its cover, but this cover was unnerving to me.

The waitress placed a drink in front of me. She glanced at the man and quickly departed.

"No, I already have one," I replied. "But thank you," I said pleasantly with a smile and turned to my drink and sucked up a gulp of it through my straw. My mother taught me always to be nice in rejecting a man's advances. That way, it wouldn't come back to bite you in the end.

"I'm Richard," he said persistently and held out his hand. I could see a gold crown on one of his teeth.

"Carrie," I said using my mother's nickname I had as a child. I felt I should give him a fake name, just in case.

He squeezed my hand and shook it. "A pleasure," he said giving me the slow once-over.

It wasn't the way he was acting; it was the look he was giving me. It gave me the chills.

There was something sinister about him. He had shifty eyes and his breath stunk something awful. That smell was the final straw. If a guy doesn't smell good when you first meet him, there's no hope for the future. I had to get away from him and fast.

I downed my drink as quickly as possible, got up, and moved away from Richard. I still could feel his eyes boring into the back of me. Man, I wanted to get out of there but not be so obvious that Richard would start to follow me.

The music changed to a rock song. I started toward the door when someone grabbed my hand and swung me around. I was terrified it was the pockmarked Richard from the bar and held my breath.

But as I looked up at the guy who was holding my hand, I relaxed. He was absolutely adorable. Young, dark tousled hair and a sweet smile on his innocent face. He was very tall. I was only five-foot-three. He must have been six-foot-two, give or take. I think he was all of twenty-five, but couldn't be sure.

"Do you want to dance?" he asked with a grin. Or was it a smirk? My guy radar was off that night.

I looked up at him but didn't answer. I was still trying to calculate his age when he leaned in toward me and cocked his head and whispered something in my ear.

"What?" I said, realizing I had not answered his question.

"Come on," he said drawing me toward the dance floor.

The music was pulsating.

He spun me around, then he pulled me closer. He was still smiling with that young face of his. His teeth were like a row of Chiclets flashing in his mouth. His generous sexy mouth. That thick dark hair. That body. That confidence only the young have. I was transfixed and maybe a little turned on. He pulled me closer and then we swayed like one. He spun me around one more time and dipped me backward, leaning toward my face. His sweet young face, those full lips, I had to get away from him before he had me in a lip lock on the floor.

"Thanks for the dance," I said and started to walk away.

He followed me.

"Let's sit down and talk," he said, guiding me over to an empty table. I was doomed.

An older waitress came over and asked him for his ID which he showed. He rolled his eyes at me as she read his driver's license.

Satisfied, the waitress asked, "What do you want to drink?"

"Beer."

She looked at me.

"A Shirley Temple," I said. I felt I had enough to drink already.

"To go with your hair?" she said sarcastically as she sashayed away.

I looked at him. He was suppressing a smile.

"To Shirley Temple!" he said smiling at me.

"To Bob Hope! He loves Shirley Temple. She calls the office all the time," I said raising my voice and looking around the room at all the booze hounds. I was ready to rumble.

"You work for Bob Hope?" he asked.

"I'm one of his secretaries," I whispered. "I have his ear," I replied pointing at my nose.

"You're cute," he smiled, wiggling his eyebrows at me.

"And you are a thousand years too young to be looking at me that way," I said trying to be the mature one.

The waitress brought us our drinks which he paid for.

She shot me a snarled look as she left.

"I like you. What's wrong with that?" he said.

"I'm too old for you."

"I like older women," he said sipping his beer, still grinning at me.

"Translation, you need a place to crash," I said.

"Maybe I can keep you warm tonight," he replied.

I rolled my eyes at him.

"What do you say?" he asked, leaning back, but still smiling.

"I have to go," I said simply and stood up hoping for a fast getaway from all the madness that night.

He stood up as well and walked me out to the parking lot. When we got to my car, I unlocked it and turned to him about to say thanks for the drink and that's when he put his arms around me and leaned in. Those youthful lips were working overtime as he slowly pressed them against my mouth. Slow was his style and he drew me in. I couldn't breathe and didn't want to. The kid of twenty-five knew how to kiss and I let him.

As we stood by the driver's side of my car, my heart was racing. I didn't want him to stop but I couldn't let him continue, so I backed away.

"Look, kid," I started, with my finger poking at his chest.

"It's Casey," he interrupted in that husky voice of his as he held onto me tightly.

He was staring down so intently at me I could hardly breathe. His eyes were sensual.

"Casey...," and he mumbled his last name. I heard the word Casey, but couldn't understand the last word, mainly because his mouth muffled the rest of the word as his lips covered mine. It was a long, passionate kiss. Casey was not that innocent as I had thought. Or maybe I was the innocent one in this picture. How could that be? I was older and thought I knew everything about everything. Tonight I knew nothing.

I also didn't notice someone was watching us, but Casey did.

It looked like Richard from the bar who was watching from the shadows about twenty feet away.

Casey glared at him. Quickly, Casey pushed me into my car and hopped into the passenger seat.

"Let's go. I don't like an audience," he said, indicating Richard who was standing in the shadows.

I frowned because I didn't like to be watched either. I started the car and quickly maneuvered it out of the parking spot. I drove to my place, all the while looking in the rear view mirror making sure Richard wasn't following us.

Maybe kissable Casey could sleep on my couch, just for tonight, I thought. Famous last words.

That one night of Casey sleeping on the couch, turned into him being in my life and turning it upside down.

As I got to know Casey better, I learned that moving ahead with his acting career was his obsession. Holy cow, I had fallen for an aspiring actor! Los Angeles was teaming with them.

Every day Casey went out searching for work in the industry, but it was so hard to break in. It usually wound up with him getting high off of weed somewhere and bringing it back to my place. For some reason the weed disappeared the next day. This happened so often I swear he was selling the stuff. Then all of a sudden Casey announced he had a lead on a potential job in Seattle. Could I float him some money, just to get started? I only had $200 which I gave to him. What can I say? I'm a sucker for a sob story and a pretty face. Casey promised he would pay me back. His last question was, did I know of any talent agents that could help him out while he was up in Seattle?

I did know a certain someone I could ask, but getting this person to agree to my request was another matter.

Chapter 51

THE FAVOR

Normally, I never ask for favors of this magnitude, because at some point, I know I am going to have to repay them in some way or fashion. However, I had told Casey I would do this for him and I didn't want to let him down. After all, I'm a woman who keeps her word.

A few days later I cornered agent Mark Anthony at the Hope house. He was the only person I knew that could make this happen.

Mark was outside waiting for Mr. Hope. As he normally would do, Mark liked to stroll around the backyard and hit a few balls onto the green to pass the time.

The phones were quiet in the Bungalow, so I slipped out the back and walked over to Mark and stood in between the path of the golf ball and the cup.

"You're in my line of sight," he said, his eye still on the little white ball.

"I have a question," I said with my arms on my hips.

"And what is that?"

"Do you know anybody in Seattle who could help a young actor?"

"A friend of yours?" he asked.

"Maybe."

"Why Seattle? I know a lot of people here in Los Angeles," he said.

"The opportunity is in Seattle and he needs someone up there," I said.

Mark stopped and I could almost see the gears moving as he was going over his many connections.

"Seattle… I might know someone. What do I get out of this?" he asked.

"The satisfaction of helping a kid on his way to becoming a star?"

He swung the club at the air practicing his golf swing.

"Not good enough," he said.

"I'll pay you," I said.

He stopped. Money has a way of doing that.

"How much?" he asked.

"Why is it always about the almighty dollar?" I asked.

"It's show business, kid. It's always about the money," said Mark.

"A hundred?" I offered.

"Get real," he smirked.

"Five hundred?"

Mark pointed the golf club up toward the sky.

"I don't have thousands of dollars to pay his seed money!" I almost shouted at Mark.

"Is he any good?"

I made a face and threw Mark a pained look. Did Mark mean at acting or something else?

"Pretty good," I said.

"Pretty? Or just good?" asked Mark with that annoying smug smile of his.

"Both."

Mark stopped his swing with the golf club in mid-air and sighed.

He pulled out his wallet and gave me a business card.

It had the name of a talent agent on it.

"Tell him to call the number and ask for Jack when he gets to Seattle," sighed Mark.

"Thank you. I'll get you a check," I replied.

I knew nothing was ever free in Hollywood.

"Forget it. Your money isn't any good with me," replied Mark.

"I thought you said…"

"Forget it. I was just messing with you," he grinned.

I stood there and then said in all honesty, "You're a very nice man, Mark."

"Just don't tell anybody. I don't want my reputation ruined."

He was bent over the ball concentrating when I dashed over to him and kissed him on the cheek and said, "Thank you."

"Only for you, doll," he said rubbing my lipstick off his face.

Neither one of us had noticed that Mr. Hope had come downstairs. Bob had been watching us as he stood near his car. Mr. Hope reached in and honked the horn.

"Hate to break up the love fest, but we gotta go!" yelled Mr. Hope.

Mark looked up and walked over to him.

As Mark passed me he whispered, "If you tell anyone, I'll kill you." Then he winked.

I nodded. Roger that.

Of course, now that I am actually telling the world about Mark, should I now be looking over my shoulder for hitmen?

Chapter 52

CHUCK AND CASEY

When I got home from the Hope Bungalow, Chuck was in my apartment arguing with Casey. Could two guys be so opposite?

Chuck was poking Casey in the chest demanding why he was with me.

Casey was taller than Chuck and held his ground. It was your typical cockfight between two guys.

I stepped into the apartment and was surrounded by both of them yelling over me.

"Will everyone take a breath! Chuck, what are you doing inside my apartment?" I demanded.

"Who is this guy?" asked Chuck still staring at Casey.

"None of your business!" shouted Casey.

I got between them. "I've got this, Casey," I said.

Chuck looked smug.

I turned to Chuck. "I want you out," I said.

"My mother doesn't allow sublets," said Chuck.

"He's not subletting. He's visiting!" I shouted.

"He has to go and now!" Chuck shouted back.

The two of them started punching each other. Casey knew Karate so it was a no-win situation for Chuck. Chuck grabbed a steak knife from the sink, which Casey easily kicked away. Glass was breaking and furniture was thrown around the room as the two of them wrestled on the floor. I grabbed Chuck and pushed him toward the door.

"Either he goes, or I go!" shouted Chuck, pointing his finger at Casey.

"Get out!" I shouted as Casey punched Chuck in the mouth, sending him flying.

Casey jumped on him and they rolled around on the floor fighting for their lives.

"My script! That's all I came for!" shrieked Chuck as the two of them crashed through my flimsy door.

I got Chuck's script and literally threw it at him. The brads came loose and all five hundred pages were in the air. I shut the door on Chuck and the flying pages.

Casey started to go after Chuck. I grabbed his arm at the door and said, "I got a number of an agent in Seattle." That stopped him.

I gave him the business card. It was a phone number of the talent agency that Mark had given me earlier.

"Why don't you come to Seattle with me?" Casey asked, grabbing onto my hand.

"I can't. Not right now," I replied. "Maybe I can visit you later?" I asked.

Casey looked sad. He had trouble finding the words to respond to me.

"It's what you wanted, Casey. Stardom, right?" I said, trying to make him feel better.

He kissed me then took the agent's card from me.

He hugged me for a long time.

"Mr. Hope's agent said this agency is always looking for fresh talent, but you would have to prove yourself," I said still holding him. "This is your shot."

He kissed me and I kissed him back. It felt like the longest kiss in history.

"I guess you should start packing," I said as I gazed into his eyes.

He nodded and asked if I could drop him at the bus station in the morning.

"No problem," I said as I grabbed his hand and led him toward my bedroom for one last romantic goodbye.

The next morning, I drove Casey to the crowded bus station.

Everyone had lined up to board the Seattle bus. Casey sweetly kissed me for the last time.

"I'll call you and let you know what happens," he said into my ear as he tightly held onto me for another minute.

I watched Casey as he got on the bus and moved toward the back. He smiled and waved goodbye to me from the rear window. He still had his hand on the window as the bus rumbled down the road. It was sad to see him leave.

I returned to my apartment and found a paper stuffed into the side of the door. Gloria, the landlord, had given me a bill for the door repair. But she never mentioned Chuck to me again.

Later that week Casey called me all excited. He had landed an acting job and was busy working on a play. He said I should visit, but I never did. I hoped he found the stardom he craved because I never heard from him again.

One thing was for certain, I think Casey had saved my life that night in the Holiday Inn parking lot.

While I was still working for Mr. Hope, I had heard the news reports about a serial killer who raped and killed women in the Glendale area. I tried not to think too much about it as I drove over to Mr. Hope's house every day. But every evening the news was reporting on someone being killed in or close to the Glendale area. It was a scary time to be living alone.

As the months rolled by, a news reporter announced that the Satan-worshipping Richard Ramirez was found to be the "Night Stalker" and had "worked" the Glendale area and other areas nearby. It was so close to my home, it gave me the chills.

Richard Ramirez had broken into several homes in the Glendale area and in April of 1984 he had killed a nine-year-old girl.

A few months later, Ramirez broke into a 79-year-old woman's Glendale home where he ultimately raped and killed her. Most of his home invasions were in 1985. At the end of August, his name and face were released to the public. I was almost sure it was the same guy that night at the Holiday Inn. A day later, a man recognized Ramirez and notified the police. Ramirez managed to steal a car, there was a chase, he got out of the car and was surrounded by an ugly crowd. They beat him until police arrived at the chaotic scene and arrested him. That was that. The system worked.

Looking back, I could have been one of his victims, one of the dead.

Maybe I only imagined that the Richard I remembered was that same guy, or it was just a weird coincidence that he looked like the killer? I can't swear to it. I just have always felt it in my bones.

And I think Casey somehow did, too.

So thank you, my sweet Casey, for being a friend when I needed one most.

Chapter 53

CELEBRATION

I don't know what occasion this celebration for Mr. Hope was for, but Mrs. Hope sure wanted all of us, the minions, out of the Bungalow at 5:00 p.m. It was like we were being kicked out of a party so the pretty people could all come in.

Celebrities from all over Hollywood came to Bob Hope's party that evening. Old Hollywood, new Hollywood, TV stars, recording stars. It was a celebration of Bob Hope.

I remember having to move my green Firebird out of the driveway because the limos were arriving by the droves. It was a Tinseltown celebration with the big, white, round spotlights moving across the sky and lighting up the night.

I wanted so badly to be a part of it but being on staff, we were the peons and had to leave.

Naturally, I did the next best thing. I parked my car farther down on Moorpark and walked back to the Bungalow.

I opened the door with the pretense of having forgotten something. Hey, it worked in the past.

It was after 5:00 p.m. and everyone was gone except the security guard who manned the gate from inside the Bungalow. He and I were friends, having bonded over the hidden woman in Bob's car. The security guard didn't care if I watched the line of cars and limos arriving. He was kept busy opening and closing the gate. His thumb sure got a workout.

That night was so glitzy and glamorous that in my mind I started to think we were at the Academy Awards.

It was dark inside the Bungalow and the Hope house and surrounding area were ablaze with lights and laughter. People were on the lawn and lights twinkled everywhere. It was so magical to me. People were drinking. Some were dancing. Where was Fred Astaire? Where was Gene Kelly? The music was lively and inviting.

I looked at the security guard and smiled. The security guard smiled back. We were in the mood to cut loose. No one was watching. The guard spun me around and around in the Bungalow. I felt like Natalie Wood in *West Side Story* (1961). Colors were blending. People were meshing. It was a dream sequence from the movies.

Fireworks were exploding outside setting off flashes of red, white, and blue colors in the sky. I heard people *oohing* and *aahing*.

I could see Armando, Mark Anthony, all the writers, Mr. and Mrs. Hope, several NBC executives, advertising executives, the two Mafia body guards, and "A" list actors from Al Pacino to Jack Nicholson, old-time stars from Dorothy Lamour to Jane Russell, former president Richard Nixon helicoptering into the backyard, Phyllis Diller, Don Rickles, Billy Barty, George Burns, Rosemary Clooney, Lee Marvin, Emmanuel Lewis, Chicago Bears football defensive lineman William Perry, Merlin Olsen, Vic Damone, George Kirby, Barbara Eden, Lucille Ball and Gary Morton, Carol Burnett, Vanessa Williams, Ann Jillian, Brooke Shields, Tom Selleck, John Ritter, Sammy

BOB HOPE'S BUNGALOW: TALES FROM THE TYPING TRENCHES

Davis, Jr., Mary Hart and husband Burt Sugarman, and a host of other movie stars from John Travolta to Tom Cruise, to The Beach Boys, and to singer Irene Cara whose song "Fame" was playing in the background.

The driveway had turned into a dance floor and everyone was dancing. Old Hollywood, new Hollywood, and more. It felt like a block party of dancers in perfect sync like in *West Side Story* (1961). The dance sequence was magical. In Toluca Lake, here they all were, the rich and the famous, moving and grooving, all celebrating Bob Hope.

I started to imagine all these people, all these Hollywood stars, spinning out of control. The room started swaying, the lights merged until one spotlight shone on Bob Hope himself at a microphone.

Bob was singing his old standard "Thanks for the Memory" to his wife, Dolores. It was so romantic, even if it was only in my mind.

I was transfixed. It was old-time Hollywood meeting the 1980s Hollywood. It was a wishful dream.

A dream which ended when the guard waved his hand in front of my face, snapping his fingers, and broke the spell. Back to reality in the Bungalow.

I smiled and said good night to the security guard who kissed my hand. Such a gentleman, I thought to myself.

Over the gate I could hear the 1972 song "Dancing in the Moonlight" by the band King Harvest. It was a catchy little tune which made me dance down the driveway.

Somehow I floated to my car on Moorpark telling myself it all had been a sweet, beautiful dream that I didn't want to end.

Tomorrow was my last day, and I had a plan to make it memorable!

Chapter 54

EXIT LAUGHING

It was finally Friday, September 28, 1984. I wanted Mr. Hope to remember me and came up with a crazy, lame-brained idea. His closing on every show was "Thanks for the Memory." It was Bob's theme song. I thought it would be cute if I said the same thing to him on my way out the door. It's not often you get to say goodbye to a star, so why not make it memorable?

That morning I called up to his room and asked when he was leaving for the flight out to his next smoker.

"It'll be later this afternoon," he said sleepily into the phone.

Must have been a rough night the evening before.

"Can you call me just before you leave? There's something I have to tell you. So just give me a quick call," I said.

He was amenable to that and said he would.

Just about every time I was on the phone with him, I reminded him that he had to call me before he left the house. Quite frankly, I kind of was a nag about it. Relentless, even. Hey, it was my one shot at this!

I made darn sure I was prepared for his call.

Let me give you just a little back story here. Every time the secretaries got a call from Mr. Hope, we hit the red "record" button on the phones. It was there for any dictation he wanted us to take down that was important or anything he wanted memorialized. Hitting the "record" button as we picked up the phone became second nature. We always had a tape in the tape recorder which was attached to the phones, so it wasn't rocket science for us to record a call.

I made sure on my last day that the tape was new and always hit the "record" button when the phone rang. I was prepared to get this down on tape. It was for me and I still have a recording of what Mr. Hope said to me.

Frances, of course, had heard my earlier conversations with Mr. Hope and was curious as to what I was up to.

Mark was already at the Hope house. He was accompanying Mr. Hope on the trip. While he waited around, he made numerous calls to his cronies.

Armando had drawn the short straw so he got to drive the two of them to the airport. He was busy polishing the Chrysler to within an inch of its life. The car gleamed and glowed like the Challenger just before blastoff.

About four in the afternoon, my phone rang and I nearly jumped out of my skin.

I had been waiting for this all day.

"Hello," I said.

"Yeah, it's me," Bob said. "You said to call, so here I am." He was on loudspeaker.

Thank God he remembered, I thought to myself as I sucked in some air.

Here goes nothing, was my other thought.

"I just wanted to wish you a safe trip and thank you for everything since it's my last day," I began.

I don't think I could have been more nervous while speaking to him.

"Oh yeah. You're going back to school, right?" Mr. Hope said.

"Yes. And here's what I really want to say to you."

There was a big pause as I took a long drag of air into my lungs.

I don't think Mr. Hope had a clue as to what was going to happen.

In my head I said to myself, Here we go.

Then I started to sing Bob Hope's old theme song, "Thanks for the Memory." I started strong and belted out the song like Ethel Merman.

"Thanks for the memory

Of sentimental verse

Nothing in my purse

And chuckles

When the preacher said

For better or for worse

How lovely it was.

Thanks for the memory

Of Schubert's Serenade

Little things of jade

And traffic jams

And anagrams

And bills we never paid

How lovely it was."

Frances, Marie and Nancy rushed over to my desk as I did this routine for Bob. They grinned from ear to ear at my awkwardness. I didn't care. Who gets to sing to Bob Hope? Needless to say, I was painfully aware that I was not a great singer.

The three of them stood around my desk with big smiles on their faces as I croaked out the lyrics. Thankfully, no one cringed.

My voice wasn't too bad, but when I started on the second verse, I began to laugh. I had been doing so well. I didn't think I was nervous, but I couldn't finish the lyrics and just broke off into nervous laughter. Forget *Star Search* (1983). I sucked!

"Oh my God, I just can't hit the high notes," I giggled into the phone to Mr. Hope.

Mr. Hope laughed with me. He still was on loudspeaker and all the girls could hear his merriment.

"That was great," he said. "Can't tell you how much I appreciated what a great job...."

Of course, silly me, I had to interrupt him in mid-sentence. Will I ever learn to keep my big mouth shut? Apparently not.

"I'm such a terrible singer," I said interrupting Mr. Hope with more anxious laughter. "What was I thinking? That I'm Ethel Merman?" I said jokingly to him.

He chuckled. "Then I'd be paying YOU to be on my show."

By now I was looking at the three smiling faces of Frances, Marie and Nancy. They were getting a big kick out of this. Not only did they hear me singing but also Mr. Hope humming along with the song. Holy cow, what nerve I had back in the day! Who does that?

"You did a great job," said Mr. Hope. "I wish you well in your studies. And good luck!"

I was grinning from ear to ear. "Well, have a great flight and I'll be seeing you on the old boob tube," I responded. Or I think that's what I said. It's all a blur now. I do know that I sang for Bob Hope and he laughed at me, or was it *with* me? I'm not sure. I hope it was *with* me.

One thing, I do know. That job working for Bob Hope for thirteen months was the best thing that had ever happened to me. I came in laughing and went out laughing. What person can say they laughed every single day at their job? Not too many secretaries get the opportunity to work for a living legend, either. Guess I was lucky.

Everyone had their own way of saying goodbye.

Armando cried and hugged me so tightly I almost stopped breathing. He also made me promise to meet him for lunch the following week, which I did. We stayed friends for years and then he retired with a nice bonus in the thousands from Bob Hope. I guess Bob liked him, too.

Mark hugged me and said to call his friend if I ever got to Vegas. Now I was crying because I realized that I'd never see Mark's pretty boy face again.

Bob and Mark were whisked to the airport by Armando. I knew Armando was upset because he nearly got into an accident leaving the driveway of the Hope house.

The girls in the Bungalow gathered around and wished me well and promised to keep in touch but they never did, which normally happens in work situations.

At 5:00 p.m., I cleaned off my desk for the last time and walked out the door toward my shiny key lime green Firebird that was waiting for me in the parking area. I think Armando was responsible for the "spit shine." He was always doing nice things like that, especially when you weren't looking.

I waved goodbye to the security guard, who blew me a kiss as a parting gesture, and I danced down the driveway to my car singing to the song, "I'm Still Standing" by Elton John.

As my green Firebird quickly flew along Riverside Drive, I started bobbing my head and singing along with a Rick Springfield song on the radio as loud as I could.

I took the 5 Freeway going east and sped back to Glendale with the music blasting from my car radio speakers.

My big, bushy hair was flying all over the place. People in other cars were gawking at me. I knew I was a sight, but I didn't care. I had just finished thirteen months working for Bob Hope and was so excited to start a new chapter in my life. It was a new day and a new dawn for me with new opportunities on the horizon. Mr. Hope was on the other side of the mountain. He had been an entertainer most of his life until he turned one hundred years old. What a great life he had lived!

Before I go, I want to officially say thanks for the memory, dear Mr. Hope, as you look down on us. Working for you was the job of a lifetime that I will never forget.

More importantly, I will never forget you, Mr. Hope, for making me laugh every single day.

Your humble Secretary # 2.

Signing off.

THE END

Bob Hope behind a seated Dolores with her dog (in black and white) circa 1970s

Bob and Dolores kissing 1998

Carol Shaw in formal attire in the 21st century

BOB HOPE'S BUNGALOW: TALES FROM THE TYPING TRENCHES

Bob Hope in golf outfit of the day as he leans on a golf club (black and white photo circa 1982)

Bob Hope and Tom Selleck circa 1983

Bob Hope's autographed picture to Carol Shaw in 1984

BOB HOPE'S BUNGALOW: Tales From The Typing Trenches

Realtor PICTURES of Bob Hope's remodeled home,
circa 2018, and Other pix

Part of the master wing
(realtor.com)

Kitchen

One of several living rooms
(realtor.com)

An elegant bar
(realtor.com)

Carol Shaw's Green Sporty 1974 Firebird (with all white leather interior) which she drove in 1983-1984 while working for Bob Hope

Carol Shaw sporting a frizzy perm of the 1980s while holding a pet dog

We were in Oslo where they say "GOD JUL"

Bob and Dolores throwing snowballs in Oslo

But here we say
"MERRY CHRISTMAS"

Bob & Dolores

(and a Happy New Year, too!)

Merry Christmas And
A Happy New Year
Bob & Dolores

Have a Merry Christmas and
A Happy and Healthy New Year!
Bob & Dolores

Dolores, Bob, and Santa in color caricatures - circa 1985

Carol Shaw

A fun Christmas card from Bob & Dolores

BOB HOPE'S BUNGALOW: Tales From The Typing Trenches

Angels Watch Over The Holy Family

della Robbia (Andrea)
15th Century
Hope Residence

May Christmas
pour its
mystery of grace
and light
on you
and those you love.

Bob - Dolores
and
Family

Bob Hope via Getty Images

www.ingramcontent.com/pod-product-compliance
Lightning Source LLC
Chambersburg PA
CBHW071715160426
43195CB00012B/1687